Worlds within a World

Reflections on Visits to Minnesota
Scientific and Natural Area Preserves

by

Paul Gruchow

field notes by Richel Burkey-Harris

Minnesota Conservation Volunteer
Minnesota Department of Natural Resources

Printing and distribution in cooperation with Minnesota's Bookstore, a unit of
the Minnesota Department of Administration Communications Media
Division, 117 University Avenue, St. Paul, MN 55155. For retail and wholesale
orders, call toll-free nationwide 1-800-657-3757, or 651-297-3000.

Design by Susan Kaneko Binkley
Map illustration by Thomas Robert Klein, Minnesota County Biological Survey
Cover photograph of Mound Prairie Scientific and Natural Area by John Gregor

Library of Congress Catalog Card Number: 99-65857
ISBN 0-9647451-3-5

Foreword

I have one of the greatest jobs in Minnesota—overseeing the protection and management of Minnesota's system of 129 dedicated scientific and natural areas. My work has involved walking land throughout the state and drinking coffee with many a landowner in pursuit of permanent protection for natural areas. My reward is to establish trust with the landowner, to acquire the land for the Department of Natural Resources Scientific and Natural Areas Program, to see the land managed for its natural value, and then to have the former owner acknowledge that the land never had so many wildflowers as when it became an SNA.

Pristine prairies, old-growth forests, peatlands—the wild back yard of all Minnesotans—have been my vocation. These special places, known by few, are open to all who respect and cherish unspoiled and untamed lands.

In this series of essays, first published in the *Minnesota Conservation Volunteer* and now collected here, author and naturalist Paul Gruchow has captured the spirit and essence of Minnesota's SNAs. To walk with Paul and see a goat prairie or bog through his eyes is memorable. From his wealth of knowledge about the past, Paul conjures up times when George Catlin and other early American explorers visited and named places such as the *Coteau des Prairies,* the namesake for Prairie Coteau SNA. As Catlin did in the early 1800s, visitors today can stride over the crest of a hill and become lost in a sea of prairie grasses and flowers.

By offering a few recollections of my visits to SNAs, I hope to provide hints of the uniqueness and mystery of these places. Perhaps such glimpses, along with Paul's vivid essays, will be enough to compel you to visit.

On a trip into Black Lake Bog SNA, Paul, SNA management assistant Tim Marion, and I dumped our canoe as we crossed the first beaver dam. Paddling out in late afternoon, after a great day exploring the bog and discussing pitcher-plants, bog-rosemary, and the merits of deerflies, we relished the thought of a cold drink and a good meal. Back at the truck, we loaded the canoe and took off. Less than a quarter of a mile down the road, the truck got a flat. As luck would have it, the rim was stuck to the drum; no amount of prying, hammering, and grousing could free it. None of us relished the thought of walking five miles to the nearest house, so we continued to work as the truck teetered on a wiggly bumper jack. Hours later, as darkness and mosquitoes descended on us, the rusted rim gave way.

On my first visit to Gneiss Outcrops SNA, I was accompanied by Ned Bray, one of the founders of the SNA Program and an expert on geology. We stood on 3.6-billion-year-old rocks in a place that bears witness to more geological history than most places in the world. The terrain is remarkably reminiscent of the Boundary Waters Canoe Area Wilderness. Instead of jack pine and blueberries, however, we found prickly pear and blue grama-grass! Years later Paul told me he had grown up in this area but had no idea this unique site existed. As Paul remarked, it is amazing how little we know of our own back yards.

Lloyd Scherer knows a lot about the 240 acres of his back yard that he gave to the people of Minnesota. His land became part of the 780-acre Lutsen SNA on the North Shore of Lake Superior. Walking this site with Lloyd, as Paul later did, I saw the affection Lloyd felt for this ecologically important piece of land covered with sugar maples and white spruce. Lutsen is an old-growth forest complex, which protects rare plants as well as old-growth trees. On a ridge here timber wolves bed down on ten-foot-deep snowdrifts, scanning the forest floor eighty feet below for movement of what could be their next meal. This scene has probably replayed for thousands of years, since sugar maples first occupied the ridge and timber wolves first used the area. It is satisfying to know they will be here still one hundred years from now, just as Lloyd intended.

Farther up the North Shore, in Lake County, is one of our newest natural areas, Iona's Beach SNA. This magical place rewards not only the eyes but also the ears. The beach is composed of tens of millions of flattened pebbles and cobbles, moved by glaciers and polished by Lake Superior for the last ten thousand years. The name of the site could have been "symphonic beach" for the tinkling sounds created when the water recedes after each successive wave and each pebble and cobble falls, slides, and rolls back into place.

Across the state in the northwestern corner is Felton Prairie SNA, which Paul visited and wrote about. In the early 1980s, I made a field trip there with two of Minnesota's premier naturalists: Dr. Walter Breckenridge, once a student of Dr. Thomas S. Roberts, the father of ornithology in Minnesota; and Art Hawkins, once a student of Aldo Leopold, the father of modern-day conservation. I drove, they talked, and I listened. Breck recalled being at this site with Dr. Roberts in the late 1920s, when chestnut-collared longspurs were as common as English sparrows. Today, in Minnesota, this rare prairie bird species is found in any numbers only in one spot along the beach ridges of Glacial Lake Agassiz. About one hundred adult longspurs still call the Felton Prairie area home.

Yet another trip was to Boot Lake SNA in Anoka County with a tour group of legislators. If you want to protect critical land, you must convince the folks who control the purse strings that what you are doing is important. Given it was a cold, windy day in April, the group opted to cut the tour short and just walk a short distance to the lake. Once at the shore, I pointed out a large white pine across the lake and told them it held the metro's first nesting pair of bald eagles. This wasn't the most impressive sight, mind you. But then, as if on cue, a bald eagle took off from another tree and flew directly at and over us. Eagles still nest at Boot Lake today, some fourteen years later, and the Legislature still supports the program. In fact, that support is stronger than ever.

Just as I have my favorite recollections of visiting Minnesota's SNAs, Paul Gruchow has his. In recalling twelve of them in this book, he introduces readers to some of Minnesota's most pristine landscapes and the important attributes they hold. More than ten times as many sites await the student of nature, the photographer, the wildflower enthusiast, the seeker of solitude.

Read one of the essays before you visit a site to see it through a naturalist's eyes. Take your time in your visit, for it is the quality of each visit that counts, not how many sites you see in a week or year. Then sleep well, knowing that Minnesota's natural areas are protected in perpetuity for all Minnesotans, and that they will be there if you return twenty-five, or even fifty, years after your first visit.

—Bob Djupstrom

Scientific and Natural Area
Essay Sites

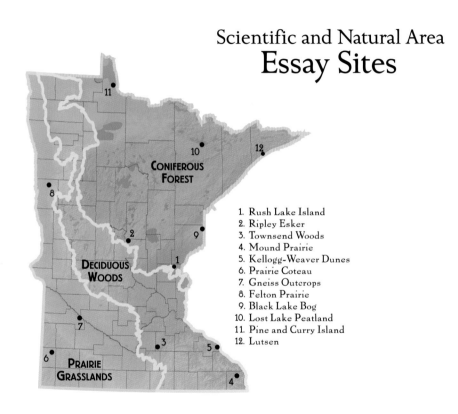

CONIFEROUS FOREST

DECIDUOUS WOODS

PRAIRIE GRASSLANDS

1. Rush Lake Island
2. Ripley Esker
3. Townsend Woods
4. Mound Prairie
5. Kellogg-Weaver Dunes
6. Prairie Coteau
7. Gneiss Outcrops
8. Felton Prairie
9. Black Lake Bog
10. Lost Lake Peatland
11. Pine and Curry Island
12. Lutsen

Detailed information on most state scientific and natural areas is available in *A Guide to Minnesota's Scientific and Natural Areas*, published by the Scientific and Natural Areas Program, Minnesota Department of Natural Resources.

Contents

Rush Lake Island Scientific and Natural Area: great blue heron nesting pair

A Joyful Noise

A single great blue heron is an imposing sight. An adult male stands four feet tall, has a wingspan of six feet, and wields a half-foot-long beak that looks more like a switchblade than a pair of mandibles. It has fierce yellow eyes with black, unflinching pupils, and a long plume floats out from the back of its head as if from a battle helmet.

The heron is a stalker, a bird that hunts its prey—fish (mostly not game fish), snakes, frogs, lizards, crayfish, insects, mice, shrews, rats. It relies on stealth and speed. It stands as still as a stone, or prowls in slow motion, or sweeps one of its improbably long toes to gently stir up whatever is lurking at the bottom of a body of water until a suitable meal comes along, and then in a flash seizes the victim in its mandibles or stabs it through, rearranges the catch bellyward, and swallows it whole. When threatened by something bigger or more powerful than it, the great blue heron goes for its attacker's eyes.

The nurseries in which the young are roosted, hatched, raised, and fledged are called rookeries. There are about 230 rookeries in Minnesota, including one on Crane Island in Chisago County's Rush Lake. The island's name reflects the common confusion of cranes with herons. The two kinds of birds are, however, easily distinguished in flight. Cranes fly with their necks extended, herons with their necks tucked in. Depending upon the year, Crane Island supports between two hundred and four hundred active great blue heron nests (once there were as many as five hundred), each containing two to four eggs. The herons, in turn, are joined by smaller numbers of nesting great egrets and double-crested cormorants. Its rookery is among the half-dozen largest in the state.

The island itself is slender and small—about twenty-three acres. At its highest point it rises just ten feet above the water. It is surrounded by bulrushes and covered with tall trees—basswoods and sugar maples, mainly, but also red oaks, silver maples, cottonwoods, ashes, and the skeletons of American elms, which were once the most common nesting sites of the herons. During the nesting season, which runs from mid-April to mid-July, the island is a raucous place.

I went to the island, now designated Rush Lake Island Scientific and Natural Area, by boat one early May day with Steve Kittelson, who works for the Department of Natural Resource's Nongame Wildlife Program. Three herons returning from an early morning fishing expedition led the way. The day was overcast and breezy. As we approached the rookery, the nests of the herons came into view: large platforms made of sticks, reeds, and whatever else happened to be available for the scrounging, including garbage and bits of plastic. The nests protruded from the highest and most exposed tree limbs in the forest canopy.

Some critters are remarkable architects, but the great blue herons are not among them. Their nests look haphazard, unkempt, and unsafe. Indeed, Kittelson said, he's seen nests so thin you could spot the eggs from below. Falls from nests are the leading killers of chicks, fewer than 40 percent of which survive their first year. Rookeries, in fact, are pretty smelly places. The chicks, when they are very young, are fed partially digested food, which their parents regurgitate into their mouths. As the young birds mature, the parents simply toss the contents of their stomachs into the nest and let the chicks fend for themselves. I saw the nests writhing and dancing from the relatively light winds. A great blue heron rookery would not be a place for a creature queasy of stomach.

We circled the little island, noting the places where there seemed to be concentrations of nests. We looked, in vain, for evidence of black-crowned night herons, a smaller and much rarer species that sometimes nests among great blues. The black-crowned herons are night feeders, the great blues day

Rush Lake Island Scientific and Natural Area: several nests on a single tree

feeders, so the association is perfectly compatible. Even without the comings and goings of the herons, the place bustled with activity. In the bulrush shallows, carp churned and splashed in noisy mating rituals. Flocks of Canada geese honked among the cattails. Along the shore, a plump woodchuck stood gazing out upon the water, looking as content as a Minnesotan with a cup of fresh coffee on the first day of a long holiday at the lake cabin.

But it was not until we beached our boat and ventured onto the island (something strictly prohibited during nesting season except with advance permission and good cause—in this case, a survey of the year's population) that the full extent of the activity in the rookery became obvious. There was, for one thing, the clamor of the herons, both the persistent clucking of the chicks and the sharp skrawking of the adults, a sound, Kittelson said, "that always reminds me of something prehistoric, like the call of an archaeopteryx." There was the abundance of the nests, seemingly one in every place where a nest might have been built. And there was the litter on the ground—the many broken eggshells, here the bones of a creature consumed, there half a fish dropped before it could be finished, everywhere the broad splashes of white guano and its strong, acrid barnyard odor.

The forest floor at the north end of the island, even so early in the growing season (the ground plants in a forest hasten to maturity before the canopy closes in and they find themselves in perpetual shadow), was nearly barren of plant life. It is there that the seventy-five-year-old rookery is now concentrated, and the accumulations of guano have substantially altered the soil. Tests on the island in 1980 showed results similar to those at other rookeries. Soils beneath the nests were much more acidic; much higher in concentrations of nitrites, phosphorus, potassium, and other soluble ions; and much less rich in organic matter than soils elsewhere on the island. And vegetation surveys confirmed the strikingly visible consequence: a dramatic drop in species diversity below the nests.

As we headed south, Kittelson picked up the half shell of a heron egg. It was perhaps slightly larger than a jumbo chicken egg and pale blue on the outside, more aquamarine than sky blue. Its interior was coated with a thin, tough off-white membrane. "This membrane is rich in blood vessels, which supply the developing embryo with oxygen," Kittelson said. "In the larger end of the egg, there is an air sac which supports the bird while it uses its egg tooth to chip its way out of the shell. Just before the birds hatch, you can hear them chirping inside the egg."

The impression of being on the island was a little like that of being contained in just such an egg. The canopy of the trees shrouded us in shade as if in a shell. The substrate at our feet was moist and just barely firm. Toads leapt away from our steps. On higher ground near the center of the island we passed the nests of geese, soft affairs shaped like broad, shallow platters. The barnyard odor of guano grew more intense as we advanced from barren earth toward land where herons historically had nested in greatest concentration. It supported a few flowers—at this season, violets, Solomon's-seals, jack-in-the-pulpits, and wild leeks. Then came a stand of dead elms and the flash of light they admitted, and the dense thickets of elders flourishing in that light. Then shadows again and muddy ground and clouds of tiny flies. Then sedge marsh. Then the water again.

Even at the edge of the water, beyond the close interior of the island, there was the cacophony of the herons, the shameless begging of the chicks, and the rattling cries of the parents, which reminded Kittelson of the Paleozoic and me of a tropical forest overrun with parrots. Sounds, at any rate, far beyond the human imagination. "My friends brought him into the kitchen," the poet James Wright said of a small blue heron,

> In a waste basket and
> Took him out and
> Set him down.
> I stroked his long throat
> On the floor. I was glad to hear him
> Croaking with terror.

Rush Lake Island Scientific and Natural Area: great blue heron with chick

I was glad, for my own reasons, to hear the din of uncivilized heron noise on Crane Island.

Kittelson set up a spotting scope, and I peered through it at the patrician head of a roosting heron. Its head plume flew wildly in the wind, but otherwise it perched as steady as a soldier at its post. Although I think the bird could not have been looking at me, its big yellow eye seemed to pierce my own. There is no way to describe the intensity of its gaze, the unblinking glare of it, so fierce I imagined it might set fires. To look into the eye of a great blue heron is to know something of the incomprehensible distance dividing herons from humans.

And then we launched ourselves into the water again among the roiling carp, whose carnal activities suddenly seemed quite mundane. A hundred yards from shore nothing was audible but the whine of the engine and the brush of the wind.

Crane Island first came into formal ownership in July 1874. The property changed hands several times over the next century. Before the turn of this century, white oaks were harvested there to be used by a local cooperage in making barrels. It was grazed by pigs and cows in the early 1900s. In the drought of the 1930s, the meadow at the south end of the island was hayed. But the island was never occupied and except at these brief intervals, rarely disturbed.

The first serious threat that the island might be developed for housing emerged in the late 1960s, just as the state was launching a new program to protect the best and most representative remaining samples of Minnesota's natural features. Heron rookeries, like living organisms, have limited lives, which can end prematurely. One good way to destroy a heron rookery is to subject it to too much human disturbance. The threat to the Crane Island rookery rather quickly came to the attention of the officials organizing the new protection effort, who soon began negotiating to buy the property. The land was acquired in 1971, and in 1974 it became the first site officially set aside as an SNA, to be perpetuated forever in a natural state.

On the way back to the boat landing Kittelson told me about another Minnesota rookery that for reasons not understood was recently abandoned. "There is no silence," he said, "quite like the silence that descends during breeding season in a place where a heron colony has been abandoned."

That such a silence has not descended upon Rush Lake is one small gift from those who crafted and have maintained the SNA Program, a gift, one might say of music—odd, inharmonious, strange music, to be sure, but vital music nevertheless in the overwhelming silence of the great universe.

Lost Colonies

In his 1932 classic, *The Birds of Minnesota*, Thomas S. Roberts described a Lake Minnetonka heron colony as one of the best known in Minnesota, "in uninterrupted existence since the lake was discovered." Roberts noted, however, that the building of homes in 1907 had spooked the birds into abandoning the site for an island nearby. He added a woeful prediction: Further development would eventually force the herons off the lake altogether.

Records show that Roberts was right. But even today nobody knows for sure what causes colonies to up and disappear.

Biologists offer plenty of speculation. Development on lake shores is a factor, removing the tall trees herons require for nesting and bringing humans into frequent contact with the colony, especially early in the season when herons are easily spooked. The loss of trees to logging, disease, or windstorms (such as the 1998 tornadoes that toppled many a nest in the Blue Lake colony of the Minnesota Valley National Wildlife Refuge) may also force herons to abandon a nesting site.

In *The Birds of North America*, Robert Butler notes that the number of breeding pairs of great blue herons in a colony correlates positively with the size of nearby wetlands, in which herons hunt for fish, frogs, snakes, and other prey. The 1987–88 Minnesota drought may have triggered the abandonment of a 58-year-old heron colony at Cold Spring Heron Colony SNA in Stearns County by reducing its amphibian population.

Other evidence suggests that predation, environmental toxins, heron droppings, and the species' weak attachment to birthplace may play a role. Droppings alter the soil, eventually killing the nesting trees. Predators such as raccoons, bears, eagles, or great horned owls may kill nestlings or adults, often triggering site abandonment. Contaminants such as PCBs, dioxins, and dieldrin may thin eggshells or kill adults, diminishing the colony's ability to sustain itself.

Further research may help scientists to both predict and enhance the stability of great blue heron colonies.

Ripley Esker Scientific and Natural Area: pasqueflowers on the ridge

Ancient River

Among the literary stars of science are the geologists. They have given hundreds of marvelous names to the language. Among the brightest constellations of these are the names describing the tracks left on the landscape by glaciers. There are moraines and tills, kettles and ice-block lakes, kames and drumlins, whalebacks and erratics, outwash fans, alluvium and drift, grooves and striations.

And there are eskers, a term inspired by the old Irish word *eiscir* for a narrow, winding ridge. When you have seen an esker, you can't imagine a better name.

A classic example is Ripley Esker, three-quarters of a mile of which has been preserved by the DNR with the assistance of the Minnesota Chapter of The Nature Conservancy. Ripley Esker SNA lies on a sand plain a few miles north of Little Falls in Morrison County, just at the edge of pine country. I visited it on one of the first days of spring.

At first glance, there seemed little to see: a modest, oak-covered ridge in an old field. But when I climbed to the top of the ridge, I found myself in a slender, grassy opening high above the surrounding plain. The ridge was only a couple of hundred feet wide at its base, and much narrower at its steep-sided apex. It snaked across the landscape like a river. There was something improbable, unreal about it, begging explanation.

An esker is, in fact, the fossilized print of a former river. About twenty thousand years ago, when Paleolithic humans were painting the walls of caves in Europe, the land around the Ripley Esker was covered by a stagnant glacier. The meltwaters of the glacier drained through a crack in the ice. As the melting quickened, the ice-bound stream grew into a surging torrent, carrying with it a load of sand and gravel. In the final stage of the glacier's dissipation, the flow in the river slowed and dropped its heavy load of sand and gravel. The river's banks of ice eventually melted away, leaving behind the riverbed just as it had been molded, serpentine, high and dry, in its own way as evocative of long ago as a fossilized nest of dinosaur eggs or an image of a bison at Lascaux.

Twice more the ice advanced, stalled, and melted away, leaving intact 6.5 miles of the ancient riverbed. The climate warmed, lichens and fungi colonized the surface rocks, a thin mantle of soil began to form. In 1853, when Father Francis Pierz, for whom the lobe of the glacier that formed Ripley Esker is named, established his mission parish for French fur traders and Ojibwe Indians at nearby Belle Prairie, the plain was a grassland and the slopes of the esker supported an oak savanna.

Fires periodically swept across the grasslands, burning up the south slope of the esker, sometimes with enough intensity to deeply scar the fire-resistant bur oaks. The scars remain today on the south sides of the trunks of a few of the old, gnarled, fantastically twisted trees that grow along the summit of the esker. I stopped to sketch one of these fire-scarred oaks, to my eye the grandest of Minnesota's native trees.

Once, many years ago, I drove through a blizzard to Collegeville, some fifty miles south of Ripley Esker, to hear the poet W. H. Auden read. Auden, then near death, showed up out of the storm, shod in a pair of absurd carpet slippers, his body contorted in the manner of a bur oak. He mumbled inaudibly for an hour or so, and shuffled off into the howling night in his flimsy slippers. But I was not greatly disappointed in the evening, having had the hour to admire firsthand Auden's large and famously furrowed and warty face. Even his cheeks had furrows. It was a face so ravaged by time, so weathered, beaten, and ugly, that it had achieved its own magnificence.

Ripley Esker Scientific and Natural Area: oaks

Only a very wise man, I wanted to believe, could own such a face.

I thought of that face again as I was sketching the oak tree, which had about it the same aura of ravaged perseverance, the same furrowed dignity.

With white settlement of Morrison County came the suppression of fire. The land was plowed and planted to crops on either side of the esker, cattle grazed its slopes, here and there a few of the choicest trees were harvested. In the new era of domesticity, life was kinder to trees, and the slopes of the esker gradually grew over into the present oak forest.

But the climate was a force that could not be suppressed. That force reveals itself today at Ripley Esker in a remarkable way. When I stood atop the esker facing east and looked to my right, I saw a remnant bur oak savanna, a prairie landscape, and beyond it an old field reverting to prairie. And when I looked to my left across the few feet of open ridge top, I saw running down the north slope of the esker a mixed hardwood forest—bur and pin oaks, paper birches, quaking aspens—a northern landscape, and beyond it, a little ice-block pond, still frozen over, drifts of snow lingering among the cattails at its edge. The esker, though only sixty feet high at its greatest elevation, functions like a mountain range, dividing the forest from the prairie with almost surgical precision. To walk the ridge is to wander simultaneously in two worlds.

I stood between those worlds at early dusk, the low sun a gauzy glow behind the thick clouds of a gathering spring rain. A great horned owl called softly, getting no answer. A hairy woodpecker flew from one perch to another, squawking noisily. The whistle of a train sounded in the distance. The last of the harvester ants descended into the nest at my feet. There was a long, deep silence.

A breeze stirred, rattling the dry leaves of the pin oaks, an icy and austere sound. One of the leaves took flight, swirling away in an air current out over the frozen pond like a butterfly. I felt a chill and zipped my jacket.

Then high overhead, invisible behind the clouds, a flock of geese honked, and somewhere to the east I could hear the quacking of ducks. Looking down at my feet, I saw in the tan prairie turf the leaves of a strawberry plant, vivid green in the dwindling light.

I stood there between the north woods and the prairie, between winter and spring, between day and night, glad to be alive in so various a world and to be present at the twenty thousandth turning of the seasons in that constant and surprising place.

The next day the esker and the green leaves of the strawberries were covered with a foot of new snow.

Red Buffalo

During the past seven years at Ripley Esker SNA, controlled burns have been slowly returning oak woodlands to oak savanna (prairie with scattered bur oaks), and old fields to prairie. With a lot of help from fire, we can restore and preserve these rare native plant communities.

Grassland wildfires, referred to as "the red buffalo of the prairie" by some American Indians, have played an important role in determining the location and persistence of Minnesota's prairies. Oak savannas such as the one found at Ripley Esker SNA depend on frequent burning for their survival. Usually perched amid Minnesota's prairie-forest transition zone, most savannas quickly succeed to forest if fire is suppressed.

This is exactly what happened when European settlers arrived in the mid-1800s. While American Indians not only permitted but also purposefully set fires (often as a way to attract or drive game), the early settlers fought prairie fires vigorously. As a result, most oak savannas disappeared, succeeding to woodlands or falling to the plow.

Recently ecologists began to recognize the critical importance of fire in maintaining prairie and savanna communities. They found that while fire kills the cambium (growing tissue) of thin-barked hardwood species such as basswood and aspen, it does not kill bur oaks because the tree's thick, corky bark protects the delicate tissue. They also found that prairie fire destroys the growing tips of many invading woody shrubs, while leaving the underground growing points of many prairie grasses and flowers untouched.

Fire returns phosphorus and other valuable nutrients to the soil, and stimulates the growth, flowering, and seed production of some prairie plant species. This results in profusely blooming and highly nutritious vegetation. The vegetation benefited grazers such as bison.

At Ripley Esker SNA, topography strongly mediates the effects of fire. The esker's drier south-facing slope burns more easily than the cooler, wetter north-facing slope. Westerly winds fan flames up the south side but have a lesser effect on the north. Elevation, wind direction, and fire combine to create dramatically different natural communities, side by side.

Townsend Woods Scientific and Natural Area: Dutchman's-breeches

A Bit of Big Woods

The Big Woods were first called that by French fur traders, and the name, apt in several ways, stuck. At the time of European settlement, the Big Woods, a maple-basswood forest, covered more than thirty-four hundred square miles along an axis stretching from north of St. Cloud through the Twin Cities, across southwestern Wisconsin and northeastern Iowa, and into Indiana.

It was a big forest not only in its extent but also in its height, the mature trees rising more than one hundred feet above the moist loam soils in which they were rooted. They formed a closed canopy so dense that, during the summer, only about 1 percent of the available sunlight reached the forest floor.

And the forest grew thickly, making passage on foot or horseback difficult and sometimes hazardous. One reminder of that danger, a granite obelisk, stands on the St. Olaf College campus in Northfield, a memorial to the Rev.

Ole O. Fugleskjel, an alumnus "who became lost in the woods … and perished from cold Dec. 6, 1909."

Most people traveled the formidable Big Woods in southeastern Minnesota by way of its rivers, one of which is the Cannon. That river's name is a study in multiculturalism: Cannon is the Anglicization of the Frenchification of the original Dakota name, which translates to River of Canoes. The Dakota Indians used the Cannon as a highway between the Mississippi River and the open prairie to the west, where they traveled to hunt buffalo.

The same fertile soils and reliable rainfall that supported the dense forest attracted farmers, who arrived in southeastern Minnesota in the 1850s. They quickly cleared the land and planted it to wheat. For a moment late in the nineteenth century, Red Wing was the biggest wheat-shipping port in the world.

Today, the largest and best remnant of the Big Woods is the square mile or so of forest that is preserved at Nerstrand Big Woods State Park. The Nerstrand forest was always an island, surrounded at the time of settlement by prairie and oak savanna. Along with their prairie homesteads, farmers obtained a parcel of woods for heating fuel and lumber.

Among the smaller but still significant remnants of the Big Woods in Minnesota are several SNAs, including Townsend Woods, near the source of the Cannon River on the western edge of Rice County. Townsend Woods, fifty acres, lies along a north-facing glacial ridge, too steep to be farmed. A creek flows through a shallow marsh at the base of the ridge, and on the ridge the forest hides a small pond.

The tall, thick tree canopy casts the forest floor into deep shade for most of the summer. The understory plants bloom in a sudden burst at the edge of spring, before the tree leaves appear and block the sunlight. These early bloomers are called spring ephemerals. One day in late April or early May, while the surrounding prairies, except for a few pasqueflowers, are still fast asleep, the first green plants emerge in the forest. A week later, they bloom, and a couple of weeks after that, the flowering season has pretty much passed. The forest floor plants are not called ephemerals for nothing. By midsummer, all evidence that most of these plants ever existed has vanished.

The flowering plants of the Big Woods floor have a certain look about them. They grow in patches, making a nearly continuous carpet. Most of them have deeply cut leaves and small white, pale pink, or lavender flowers, often star-shaped. Most of them get to be no more than a few inches tall. From a distance, these carpets of lacy plants scattered on the forest floor give the appearance, as in a Victorian parlor, of so many antimacassars—those small covers placed on the back and arms of upholstered furniture to prevent wear and soil.

The flowers of the Big Woods include spring-beauties, wood anemones,

Townsend Woods Scientific and Natural Area: hepatica and false rue-anemone (crowfoot family)

false rue-anemones, rue-anemones, Dutchman's-breeches, bloodroot, wild ginger, toothwort, sharp-lobed hepaticas, nodding trillium, swamp-buttercup, marsh-marigold, and two species of trout lilies—the common white-flowered one and the Minnesota dwarf trout lily, indistinguishable from the white trout lily except when its tiny, faintly pink blossom briefly emerges. The dwarf trout lily is among the rarest plants in the world, surviving, so far as anybody knows, only in remnants of the Big Woods in Rice, Steele, and Goodhue counties. It is the only plant endemic to the state.

Many of the flower species of the Big Woods are members of a single family, the crowfoot, thought to be among the oldest of the flowering plants. Some plants of the forest floor are even older: fungi, ferns, horsetails, mosses, which multiply by producing spores rather than seeds, as plants did before the evolution of flowers.

Though ornamented with plants of venerable lineage, the Big Woods is only about three hundred years old. When the climate suddenly became warmer and wetter, it emerged where once oaks had dominated.

Because the spring flowering happens so quickly, I had been monitoring the Big Woods every few days. One weekend the flowers seemed to be two to three days away from their peak. Other obligations intervened and a week passed before I got to Townsend Woods. When I finally arrived, I found a patch of Dutchman's-breeches or wood anemones still in bloom here and there. Yellow violets and nodding trilliums, somewhat slower bloomers than the other spring flowers, were in full flower. But the flowering season was almost over. The dense canopy of the tall trees was already closing in.

As I walked through the forest, I heard indistinctly a sound I could not place, high and shimmering. The sound of baby birds, I thought at first, but more like squeals than chirps. I scanned the canopy for a clue to its source and did not find one. My eye was drawn instead to a hollow high in a sugar maple tree. I scanned it with my binoculars, wondering whether it was occupied. I saw nothing and prepared to move on, when an odd glimmer of whiteness registered in my brain. Taking up the binoculars, I looked again, and this time I recognized the facial mask of a raccoon, and then I could see its eyes staring out at me. We scrutinized each other for several seconds. Distracted by the scolding of a gray squirrel, I glanced away for an instant, and when my eyes returned to the hole, the face was gone. But from inside the maple, I heard once again the sound that had stopped me. This time I recognized it as the puppyish whimpering of a litter of baby raccoons.

Later, I sat on the trunk of a fallen tree up the ridge from a woodchuck's den. From there I had a view of the creek and the pond in the valley below and, high in the canopy, of a big nest, possibly occupied by a pair of great horned owls. For a quarter of an hour or so as I sat there, an unnatural silence prevailed. Gradually, as I took my place in the forest, the stir of late afternoon activity resumed.

Across the pond, one of the great blue herons roosting in a dead tree left its perch and came down to the water to stalk for dinner. A pair of wood ducks swam into view, clambered onto a tiny island, and preened. Chorus and leopard frogs called. A white-breasted nuthatch worked the trunk of a red oak. A bumble-bee, which had been collecting nectar from a late-blooming patch of Dutchman's-breeches, droned past me, landed, then disappeared into its chamber in the forest floor. A painted lady butterfly flitted by. A wood thrush began robustly to sing. *Ee-o-lay,* it sang in its luscious, flutelike voice. *Ee-o-lay! Ee-o-lay!*

A flurry of motion about thirty yards down the slope caught my eye. I looked and saw an eastern chipmunk perched on the upturned roots of a fallen tree. I suppose that there is not a more beguiling denizen of these woods. A chipmunk is quintessentially cute—pert, petite, bright-eyed, and curious, a Walt Disney creature if ever there was one.

Then I saw that the chipmunk was chewing on something as long and lithe as a length of rope. I raised my binoculars for a closer view and was astonished to see that the little animal was eating a garter snake more than a foot long and

Townsend Woods Scientific and Natural Area: the omnivorous chipmunk

as big around as my index finger. It held the snake in its forelegs like a piece of licorice and, beginning at the head end, snarfed it down, bones and skin as well as flesh, picking away at the entrails when it reached them, as you or I might dig out the last morsel of a lobster's claw.

When nothing remained of the snake but a little scrap of belly skin, the chipmunk fastidiously cleaned its paws and jowls and, its toilet completed, disappeared into its den in the tree roots, no doubt to sleep off its orgy.

I went down to examine the scrap of snakeskin, just to confirm that I had not been lulled, in the lazy ambience of the late afternoon forest, into a daydream.

When I got home, I looked up eastern chipmunks in Evan B. Hazard's *The Mammals of Minnesota*. "They are known," I read, "to take small bullfrogs, red-bellied snakes, robins, juncos, house sparrows, starlings, and meadow voles. In Michigan, I saw an eastern chipmunk take a nestling cardinal despite vigorous harassment by the parents. Although chipmunks are certainly not as efficient predators as weasels (which are about the same size), they are several times more numerous and may well be equally significant predators on populations of various animals."

Hazard adds, "Chipmunks are a source of much enjoyment, though people often have an unrealistically benign image of the personalities of these aggressive, often antisocial rodents."

There it was, another illusion shattered.

When I thought about it, I realized that that is one of the reasons I find myself mesmerized by the natural world. Whenever you are tempted to make something treacly of it, nature conspires to show to you its tart reality. Nature is not, as it is so often represented, an escape from anything, but a bracing call to realism.

So I was not surprised, when I looked *treacle* up in the dictionary, to find where the word came from. It once referred not to something cloyingly sweet, as it does now, but to an antidote to poisonous bites. It was derived from an ancient Greek word meaning "wild animal," the same root that gave us the word *fierce*.

Fierce, for example, as a chipmunk.

Wild Strategies

Each wildflower adopts a different strategy for survival. Consider these wildflowers of Townsend Woods SNA.

The word *wildflower* often calls to mind something like the spring-beauty *(Claytonia virginica)*. Its delicate pink-striped, white or pink flowers sit atop equally delicate stems and leaves. Patches of spring-beauties carpet the ground in early spring, taking full advantage of the sunlight still reaching the forest floor. When the forest canopy fills out and shades the understory, the flowers die and the visible plant disappears. Underground, however, a chestnutty-tasting tuber—food for Indians, early pioneers, and black bears—lies dormant in winter and sends up a new shoot the next spring.

Another Big Woods wildflower takes a different tactic. One of Minnesota's forty-three native orchid species, putty root *(Aplectrum hyemale)* was named for the use of its ground-up root as a cohesive in pottery making. The plant bears a single, green and white-striped leaf, as papery and crinkled as a Chinese lantern. This leaf appears in autumn, survives winter and spring, and withers away in summer when the overhead canopy fills out. Then the plant sends up a white, nonphotosynthetic stalk bearing six to sixteen flowers: green and purple-tinged sepals protecting small, whitish petals. The timing seems odd, but DNR botanist Welby Smith believes the plant is conserving its energy. Its photosynthetic leaf disappears once the overhead canopy is full; the nonphotosynthetic stalk appears when the stiff competition among spring ephemerals for pollinators has abated.

The ubiquitous wild ginger *(Asarum canadense)*, with its fuzzy petioles and broad, heart-shaped leaves, adopts yet another strategy. Its flower is actually a set of thick maroon to brown sepals forming a cup that lies close to the ground, often under the leaf litter, where marauding millipedes and ants can reach it. The flower's odor of rotting meat attracts gnats and flies, which help carry pollen from one plant to the next. Ants carry away the seeds but eat only the coats, dropping the rest at some distant location. Instead of being showy or sweetly scented for the birds, bees, and butterflies, this homely, foul-smelling flower does its essential work nearly in the dark.

Mound Prairie Scientific and Natural Area: bird-foot violet

Goat Prairie Patchwork

The word *prairie* evokes images of flatness, endlessness, featurelessness. This impression is so powerful that even the people of prairie places are often portrayed—for example, in the film *Fargo*—as flat, dull, emotionless.

But prairies are no more predictable than people, and they come in almost as many guises. The Flint Hills of Kansas, the Sandhills of Nebraska, the Loess Hills of Iowa, the butte and badlands country of the western Dakotas are not flat, but they are prairies. The cedar glades of Missouri, the aspen parklands of northwestern Minnesota, the oak savannas of southern Wisconsin are not treeless, but they too are prairies. So are the watery labyrinths of the Cheyenne Bottoms in north-central Kansas, the Rainwater Basin in southeastern Nebraska, the prairie pothole region of the north-central plains, although they harbor more ducks and cattails than grasses.

"Horizontal grandeur," as Bill Holm felicitously put it, is one aspect of the prairie landscape, but it is hardly the only one. If you want to stretch your sense of what a prairie is and if you have strong legs and lungs, visit one of the goat prairies of southeastern Minnesota.

Goat prairies are so called, not because you'll find any goats on them, but because they are the sorts of places goats might love—rocky, extremely steep, exposed. They occur on river bluffs, often south or west facing, where summertime conditions are too hot and dry to support forests and where fires, in the days when fire still shaped the landscape, once burned freely. Lightning sparked fires, and before European settlement, Indians set fires to maintain openings in the otherwise densely forested hills of southeastern Minnesota—places where game animals, vital in a hunting and gathering economy, might prosper. So these goat prairies are both natural and cultural artifacts of the region.

I visited a particularly fine goat prairie, Mound Prairie SNA, one late spring day with Bob Djupstrom, who manages Minnesota's SNA Program. The site lies just east of Houston, in the valley of the Root River. The forecast was for sunny skies and temperatures in the low eighties, but the season had been cantankerous, and the day actually proved to be heavily overcast and foggy with temperatures in the middle fifties, perfect weather for all the climbing necessary to see a goat prairie.

From State Highway 16 in the river bottom, the massive, trapezoid-shaped hills, with their crowns of oaks like cockscombs, looked brown and still asleep. This was not surprising. Because of the persistent coolness, everything in the natural world was a bit behind schedule. In any case, all prairies in which the dominant plants are warm-season grasses are late sleepers.

Rather than tackling the goat prairie directly from the base of its steep slope, we approached it on the gentler incline of an old logging road along the forested backside of the hill. The forest is dominated by northern pin oaks, handsome, sturdy trees, straight of trunk and many-branched. Oaks as a family are generally broad of limb, but the branches of the pin oaks, given to graceful downward curves, are delicate, needlelike—hence their common name. Hence too their salvation: So many branches make for knotty lumber. Except as firewood, pin oaks have little commercial value.

The leaf buds of the oaks were just opening. They were the size of a squirrel's ears. Djupstrom reminded me of the folk wisdom that when the leaves of the oaks are the size of a squirrel's ears, it is time to gather morel mushrooms. Not a minute later, we came across a perfect morel specimen standing above the leaf mold on the forest floor, flesh colored and glistening like a disembodied brain.

Where the forest had been grazed, an understory of northern prickly ash, shrubby trees as hostile to intruders as cactuses, barred the way. We circled

Mound Prairie Scientific and Natural Area: shooting-stars and bastard-toadflax

through open woods where the shrubs were Juneberries and pin-cherries. Their white flowers appeared to hang in the misty forest like low-lying clouds.

The air was bright with bird song. *Drink your teaeee,* a rufous-sided towhee called. Indigo buntings bantered, their songs bouncing through the valley like marbles. Robins chattered, warblers warbled, a lark sparrow trilled and buzzed. A ruffed grouse thumped like a kettle drum.

We came out onto the prairie, an open sweep of hillside so steep that we had to mind our steps to keep our footing.

The grassland that had looked asleep at a distance was very much awake and awash in delicate color. Tens of thousands of bird-foot violets and prairie violets bloomed in shades of sky blue, setting off tens of thousands of creamy yellow lousewort flowers, the feathery basal leaves of the plants as green as new peas. Scattered among these were the tiny but vivid blossoms of the blue- and yellow-eyed grasses, the golden flowers of the hoary puccoons, and the elegant white blossoms of a plant with a decidedly inelegant common name, bastard-toadflax.

In the shady crevices of limestone outcrops, the first scarlet and yellow blossoms of the columbines and the pale yellow trumpets of the nodding bell-worts had opened. A colony of shooting-stars made a brilliant splash of purple. Among these flowering plants were the silvery gray leaves of young scurf-peas,

Mound Prairie Scientific and Natural Area: timber rattlesnake

the pewter-gray leaves of leadplants, the forest-green needles of junipers, and the wine-colored and tan foliage of last summer's tallgrasses. The effect in the soft morning light was of an immense oriental carpet, mellowed with great age, spread opulently across the hills.

The first bloom of the season, we noticed, had already passed. Pasqueflowers open soon after the snow has melted. When the plant has finished blooming, its leaves emerge. At the same time, the stems of the ground-hugging blossoms lengthen, elevating the seed heads into the spring breezes. By the time the taller prairie plants have sprouted and begun to cast the surface of the soil into shadow, the pasqueflowers are returning to the dormancy in which they spend most of each year, having finished in a few weeks the work that it takes some plants several months to accomplish.

Among the nearly slumbering pasqueflowers, we found the new growth of many plants that bloom later in the season. A prairie achieves the ideal that every gardener with a perennial border seeks: a continuous succession of flowers from frost to frost. In fact, many of the plants that we found are the wild relatives of cultivars common to midcontinent gardens. We saw blazing stars, coneflowers, coreopsis, goldenrods, saxifrage, and Indian-paintbrush.

We found the young growth too of several rare plants that thrive on Mound Prairie, including goat's-rue, prairie wild indigo, Ohio spiderwort, and the rarest of them, the narrow-leaved milkweed, endangered in Minnesota, where it survives only on this prairie.

The site is also home to a couple of uncommon animals, the prairie vole, otherwise known in the state only farther west, and the timber rattlesnake, which has been hunted nearly to extinction. This shy snake survives at Mound Prairie in such numbers that occasionally a person encounters one on the golf course that abuts the preserve.

It was jacket weather, inhospitable to the cold-blooded snake, but we wandered up and down the slopes, peering into limestone crevices anyway, in the vain hope we might chance upon one.

As we searched, the fog lifted, and we were left not with an image of a persecuted creature, but of a place where the wild and the domestic reside in proximity. We saw flower-covered hills, masses of trees delicately green with new leaves, and below us a green valley with a ribbon of river and one of highway, wending among tidy farmsteads and cultivated fields that hugged the graceful contours of the land. We heard the songs of birds mingling with the exasperations of golfers. If there was a handsomer place on earth, we did not know at that moment where it might be found.

Our Prairie Biome

Perhaps miraculously, Minnesota still contains fragments of the once vast prairie biome that stretched diagonally from the state's southeastern tip to its northwestern corner. These fragments represent a multitude of different prairie communities, some of which shelter as many as 350 plant species.

Moisture levels generally decrease to the west, favoring dry, or shortgrass, prairies. Temperatures generally are cooler to the north, favoring the encroachment of brush and trees. Most areas support a mixture of prairie types, depending on local factors such as topography, fire frequency, soil types, temperature, and rainfall.

Scientists classify prairie communities first by moisture availability, from dry to mesic to wet. They identify these prairies by their dominant grasses: little bluestem *(Schizachyrium scoparium)* and side-oats grama *(Bouteloua curtipendula)* for dry prairie, big bluestem *(Andropogon gerardii)* and Indian-grass *(Sorghastrum nutans)* for mesic prairie, and prairie cord-grass *(Spartina pectinata)* and blue-joint *(Calamagrostis canadensis)* for wet prairie. They identify other types, such as dry oak savanna, mesic brush prairies, and wet brush prairies, according to their higher percentages of brush or tree cover.

Dry prairie can be divided into subtypes based on underlying landforms. The barrens subtype, for example, occurs on deep glacial river sand deposits. Sand-gravel prairie grows on glacial lake or meltwater deposits, and the hill prairie on steep slopes of loamy glacial soil. The bedrock bluff subtype, or "goat prairie"— such as that found in Mound Prairie SNA— occurs along steep river bluffs over bedrock.

Sedges (with edges), rather than grasses, dominate the calcareous seepage fen, a unique prairie community where cold groundwater continuously saturates soils, so that slow decomposition causes the buildup of dead plant material called peat.

Across the prairie biome, many prairie types intermix and intergrade to form complex prairie ecosystems. These ecosystems provide habitat for species that would not survive in small, isolated patches. Conservationists today work to protect not only isolated prairie remnants, but also the larger landscapes needed to ensure these species' survival.

Kellogg–Weaver Dunes Scientific and Natural Area: blowouts

Shifting Sands

It is a modest claim to fame, to be sure, but I now happen to be acquainted with both Minnesota species of fameflower, not only the comparatively common one *(Talinum parviflorum),* which grows on rock outcrops in western Minnesota, but also the endangered one, rough-seeded fameflower *(T. rugospermum),* which grows in sandy midwestern places.

Where the name fameflower comes from, I cannot imagine. The rare species was first reported in 1832 at Taylors Falls by the naturalist on Schoolcraft's expedition to search for the Mississippi headwaters, but the plant was not recognized and described as a new species until 1899.

DNR botanist Ellen Fuge, who had seen the endangered plant before, and I, who hadn't, were on the watch for it when we visited Kellogg–Weaver Dunes SNA near Kellogg one mid-July day. Not until we stopped and got down on our hands and knees to examine something else—maybe one of the punkishly iridescent beetles that seemed to be everywhere that day—did the fameflower reveal its presence. It stands all of an inch or two high; has narrow, succulent leaves of no particular distinction, although of a pleasing shade of green; and fades into the crowd of larger and showier plants all around it.

The rough-seeded fameflower was not blooming when we saw it, but we could hardly have expected it to, since it was still morning. Its odd habit is to bloom only between three and six in the afternoon, provided the sun is shining. In this, the rough-seeded fameflower is readily distinguishable from its more common cousin, which blooms from noon until three. One alternative common name for the fameflower, which I prefer, is flower-of-the-hour, in honor of this peculiarity. Presumably its blooming time suits the habits of its pollinators, discourages the advances of unwelcome suitors, or in some other way serves its interests; but what the particulars are, nobody knows. While science flourishes at the theoretical level, and technology razzles and dazzles, a billion details remain to be learned about basic natural history—work for inquisitive amateurs everywhere.

The fine, tan sands of Kellogg–Weaver Dunes occupy a terrace formed by the Mississippi River during the last ice age. From a distance, they appear to be just another low line of hills nestled among the river bluffs. But when you approach them on foot, these grass-covered and flowery hills reveal a different character.

The hills themselves prove to be rather sharply ridged. The ridges follow the north-northwest to south-southeast line of the prevailing winds. Walking across their soft surfaces is a little like walking on thick carpet. The depressions between the hills are bowl-shaped. There are blowouts, places where the sands are on the move. Since the original land survey of 1855 does not report blowouts, ecologists think grazing livestock set the sand in motion. The few plants that have taken root in the blowouts creep along the sand, making little green doilies rather than standing erect. The delicate, long leaves of sand reed-grass, blowing back and forth in the wind, have etched their circular paths in the sand.

Even where the dunes have stabilized, the plants are widely spaced, leaving a good deal of the surface exposed. In these exposures, mosses and British soldier lichens flourish. With their tiny but loud scarlet fruiting bodies, the lichens look, indeed, with a dollop of imagination, like ranks of toy soldiers.

I love that name—British soldier lichen. So many of our plant names are dutiful and literal in their descriptiveness, strictly utilitarian. A bit of metaphorical fancy makes both name and object memorable—the prime purpose, I suppose, of a name. Fanciful names encourage us to see the lives around us in a friendlier, more playful, and less relentlessly exploitative way.

On the north- and east-facing slopes of the dunes, stands of black oak, hack-berry, green ash, and aspen have taken root, creating a mosaic of sunshine and

Kellogg–Weaver Dunes Scientific and Natural Area: Blanding's turtle

shade, of sand prairie and savanna. Chokecherries, wild plums, sumac, poison ivy, and dogwood grow in thickets at the edges of these woods. The lowest and wettest areas contain shrub thickets of chokecherry, plum, juniper, and aspen. The landscape is also dotted with red cedars, a naturally occurring but aggressive species once controlled by wildfire. Today the DNR attempts to control the cedars by burning and cutting. On the horizon beyond the SNA, you see jack and red pine plantations—pines being, along with melons, among the few agricultural crops that thrive in these sandy soils.

To the east of the dunes spread the marshy backwaters of the Mississippi. Marshes and sandy grassland in close proximity constitute the ideal habitat for the threatened Blanding's turtle (easily identified by the prominent yellow throat), which ranges widely from Nebraska to Michigan. Perhaps the country's largest concentration of them survives in these Mississippi backwaters. In recent years the DNR has marked and released more than twenty-three hundred Blanding's turtles in the vicinity of the dunes.

Early in the spring, the female turtles rise up out of the marshes and travel considerable distances, sometimes more than a mile, into the dunes, moving at glacial speed, to dig their nests and lay their eggs in the sand. Along one frequently traveled pathway, they must cross a paved county road to get to the dunes. A Rare Turtle Crossing sign marks the route.

The turtle's journey to the dunes is arduous and dangerous. The many fragments of whitening turtle shell scattered in the sand are proof of that. The tattered shells of turtle eggs eaten before the hatch also litter the dunes. Barely buried in the sand, the eggs are not difficult to locate and many predators find the eggs delectable. When a tiny Blanding's hatchling does emerge from its nest, it still has to make its defenseless way across the sands to the water, potential prey to predators attacking from land and air. How a hatchling finds its way to the marsh is another mystery awaiting an explanation.

I have sometimes said, watching anxiously over my own children, that every human infant who makes it to maturity is a miracle. The maturity of a Blanding's turtle is that miracle compounded. The turtle species endures because its females lay hundreds of eggs during their long lifetimes. They play the averages. But this ancient strategy for survival can be undone by the loss of habitat, a threat compounded when the species occupies, as does the Blanding's turtle, a rather narrow and uncommon niche in the environment. The SNA offers a lifeline to this gentle and beautiful creature, as it does to many other species less likely to evoke human sympathy. Snakes, for example.

The desertlike duneland looks like snake country, and it is. The dunes are home to Minnesota's largest snake, the bullsnake, listed as a species of special concern. Ordinarily a placid creature and, for this reason, in demand as a pet, the bullsnake is capable of striking out at an intruder when cornered and is heart-stopping because of its size, which may reach six feet. When threatened, it hisses loudly and vibrates its tail, making the convincing case that it is, although harmless, a rattlesnake.

Two other harmless snakes in demand for the pet trade, the eastern and western hognose snakes, also occupy the dunes. Both are listed as species of special concern in the state. Both species have spectacular talents as actors, although the eastern hognose is superior in this regard. When provoked, a hognose snake will coil up, hiss, and spread the sides of its neck, making itself appear a good deal more formidable than it actually is. If this ploy fails, it will writhe about, exuding drops of blood from its teeth. If the Dracula act fails, the snake will flop belly up and go limp—a schmaltzy impression of death.

The racer is another species of special concern jeopardized by over-collection for the pet trade. Blue gray or light brown above, bluish white or pale yellow below, the racer is long, slender, sleek, and swift. It is a handsome creature, if you can accept the idea of handsomeness in snakes.

Jumping spiders live here too. They constitute the largest family of spiders. They do not spin webs to catch their prey—they are hunters rather than trappers. Eighteen of the sixty or so species of jumping spiders known to occur in Minnesota have been found on or near Kellogg–Weaver Dunes SNA, the most diverse assemblage of them in the state. Eight of them are included on the state list of species of special concern.

You could make a rich and engaging anthology of folk stories about spiders, ranging across cultures, continents, and ages. However, relative to their numbers and importance on earth, we pay little attention to invertebrates of any kind, to the impoverishment of the human imagination.

An exception, perhaps, are butterflies. There is a threatened butterfly on the Kellogg–Weaver Dunes, the ottoe skipper, a creature of oak savannas. But there are also, happily, legions of more common butterflies, including the regal fritillary, that bright emissary to virgin grasslands and wet woodland meadows from the Rocky Mountains to Maine. When I was on the dunes in mid-July, the regal fritillaries were everywhere by the hundreds or thousands—big, red-orange, black, and white butterflies. They darted left and right, high and low, never resting anywhere for more than a second or two, showering the land-scape with vivid light.

In several cultures, butterflies are said to be the souls of humans, risen from mortality. If they are not actually souls incarnate, the regal fritillaries at Kellogg–Weaver Dunes are, at the least, a hopeful and energetic symbol of a rare and dwindling natural community with a lease on the future.

Dune Life

A blanket of coarse sands, silts, and clays up to 150 feet thick lies atop Paleozoic bedrock at Kellogg–Weaver Dunes SNA. Only a select suite of species can survive the dry, sandy, low-nutrient environment. Even fewer can withstand the extreme conditions of a blowout, where winds create shifting patches of bare sands, often atop the highest dune ridges.

One of these hardy pioneers is false heather (*Hudsonia tomentosa*). This woody evergreen shrub, up to six inches high, occurs only in blowouts. Its small, scaly, juniperlike leaves, along with a covering of dense hairs, reduce the amount of moisture lost by evaporation. The leaves also resist abrasion by blowing sands. Amazingly, false heather can survive being buried up to its neck in sand, as long as a few leaves stick above the surface. Its extensive root system anchors the plant and takes advantage of any available precipitation or groundwater.

Once false heather establishes itself, it can provide a protected center in which other species become established. One is the tall, robust sand reed-grass (*Calamovilfa longifolia*). Two others, sea-beach-needlegrass (*Aristida tuberculosa*) and purple sand-grass (*Triplasis purpurea*), are considered rare in the state, confined as they are to Minnesota's little-known dunes.

These dunes developed from sands deposited by Glacial River Warren about ten thousand years ago, as it drained the giant Glacial Lake Agassiz. Much later, the Mississippi River cut down through the sandy floor the river had left behind to form a nine-mile long, 1½-mile wide terrace, named Teepeeota Point, which is now situated high above the river. The south end of the terrace is Kellogg–Weaver Dunes SNA.

Dakota Indians once hunted and fished from the terrace. Droves of elk and buffalo likely grazed the sandy prairie. In 1855 Irish farmers planted melons and other crops there and grazed horses and cattle. Scientists believe that the combined effects of grazing and wind destabilized the prairie sands and caused blowouts.

Prairie Coteau Scientific and Natural Area: divide between Mississippi and Missouri watersheds

Coteau des Prairies

Challenged to choose the single word that best describes prairies, you might well say "flat." Hurtling along in a car at sixty miles per hour, the modern traveler is most impressed by the prairie landscape's relentless sameness: its big skies, long horizons, straight roads following the cardinal directions, the tidy geometry of farm fields, and the limited palette of soothing colors.

Ironically, Minnesota's few remaining native prairies survive in rough and hilly places: on the beach ridges of Glacial Lake Agassiz in the northwest, on the high slopes of river bluffs in the southeast, on land too steep or rocky to be plowed in the southwest. They tend to be very dry or very wet. The richest and most representative prairies—those on level black-loam soils that yielded the richest agricultural region on earth—have all but disappeared.

Among the most dramatic of the surviving prairie remnants are those in southwestern Minnesota and eastern South Dakota on the *Coteau des Prairies,* the Highland of the Prairies, aptly named by the early French explorers and fur traders who visited the region (and who also gave us the word *prairie)*. Later explorers included Joseph Nicollet, leader of government-sponsored expeditions in 1838 and 1839 to map the territory between the Mississippi and Missouri rivers. Although he had been told the territory was "an utter desert," except along the banks of the Minnesota and Des Moines rivers, Nicollet was much taken by the beauty and variety of the landscape he encountered. He was especially moved by the prairies as he saw them from the Coteau.

"There is almost always a breeze over them," he wrote. "The security one feels in knowing that there are no concealed dangers, so vast is the extent which the eye takes in; no difficulties of road; a far spreading verdure, relieved by a profusion of variously colored flowers; the azure of the sky above, or the tempest that can be seen from its beginning to its end; the beautiful modifications of the changing clouds; the curious looming of objects between earth and sky, taxing the ingenuity every moment to rectify;—all, everything, is calculated to excite the perceptions, and keep alive the imagination. In the summer season, especially, everything is cheerful, graceful, and animated. The Indians, with herds of deer, antelope, and buffalo, give life and motion to them. It is then they should be visited; and I pity the man whose soul could be unmoved under such a scene of excitement."

Nicollet's way of looking at the landscape has, of course, become obsolete. When I visit Prairie Coteau SNA near Pipestone, a 327-acre remnant of what Nicollet saw, I, like Nicollet, do so without any anticipation of danger; I know perfectly well that no belligerent bear lurks in one of the site's deep ravines; I expect no surprise encounter with potentially hostile residents. Difficulties of road are pretty much limited to the unlikely possibility that my car might break down along the highway that skirts the site and that it might be twenty or thirty minutes before I could summon help. The terrain itself will present no surprises; I carry with me maps detailing the topography of the place, its vegetation, its agricultural history, its history of development and disturbance, its prairie management history, and its ownership. As for the animation in the landscape, the nomads, both human and animal, have long since departed from the place. The nearest antelope is now several hundred miles westward, the last elk were seen in the neighborhood in 1911.

Should I fail here to feel as excited as Nicollet did, I doubt that this failure would confirm the unhappy state of my soul as much as it would reflect an inevitable change of perspective. Excitement is an explorer's word. Yet the Coteau continues to work its magic.

By the time you reach southwestern Minnesota, you have already begun to perceptibly climb the long incline to the base of the Rocky Mountains. Without

Prairie Coteau Scientific and Natural Area: small white lady's-slipper

being quite conscious of how or where it has happened, the landscape, as you head west, opens up, expands—the skies explode. You have the sensation of being on a summit, inexplicable because all around you the same flat land extends into the distance.

And then the Coteau itself suddenly floats upon the horizon. It is technically a terminal moraine, a region where the gravel and stone carried down from the north by the glaciers of the last ice age were dumped as the climate warmed and the ice retreated. This happened when farming—a force on the landscape in its own way as powerful as the glaciers—was just being invented, thousands of miles distant, to the south, to the east, to the west.

From the perspective of ten or twenty miles, the Coteau looks like a range of vaguely blue mountains, though it is less than two hundred feet high. On the prairies, as Nicollet said, objects do loom preternaturally. And then, as suddenly as these highlands appear on the horizon, they disappear, as mountains do, swallowing you up in a labyrinth of narrow ravines and coulees.

The SNA lies along the northeastern edge of the Coteau. It is a remnant of glacial till hill prairie, a threatened community in Minnesota. Too hilly ever to have been plowed, the land was used as pasture for a century.

The parking lot at the site faces a steep hillside that has not been grazed since 1970. A little sedge meadow thrives at its base, home to southwestern Minnesota's largest population of small white lady's-slippers, a prairie orchid once abundant across much of the northeastern United States. Slow growing and long lived, white lady's-slippers are now reduced from their original numbers by 99 percent because of lost habitat.

Without moving more than a hundred yards from the parking lot, you might spot an upland sandpiper or a rare skipper butterfly or a prairie moonwort, a tiny fern that grows no more than three or four centimeters high. You would have seen the Coteau then, but you would not yet have experienced it.

To do that, you must climb the hill. Don't hurry. Sit down somewhere up the slope and catch your breath if you have to. Sit down even if you don't have to catch your breath. Prairie watching is not an athletic event, and many of this grand landscape's best features, paradoxically, are visible only close at hand.

I'll never forget a prairie tour led by Hugh Iltis, the great botanist at the University of Wisconsin, discoverer of the parent plant of corn. Everyone in the tour group was a die-hard prairie enthusiast, and many were distinguished scientists themselves. What mysteries of taxonomy would Iltis reveal? What fine points of prairie botany would invite his attention? We all followed him a little way into the prairie.

"Now," he said, turning to address us, "I'd like you all to find a comfortable spot and lie down. Flat on your backs, please. And remain there. I'll tell you when it's time to go on."

We were a bit embarrassed to engage in this childish exercise, but we did as we were told. Iltis was, after all, a renowned scientist. Five minutes passed, and then ten. We were at first self-conscious and then somewhat bored. We had come to be instructed, not to lie around in the grass. Iltis, flat on his back in his own spot, paid us not the slightest notice. He seemed to be caught up in some private reverie. Then, as we lay there, the prairie began slowly to come alive. We were aware of the slight breeze rustling through the tall grasses, of the delicacy and striking beauty of tiny grass flowers, of the aroma of sage and mint, of the extraordinary variety of insects flitting and crawling everywhere, of the lichens and mosses at the bases of flowering plants and grasses, of the searing intensity of the afternoon sun.

We lay there a quarter of an hour before Iltis finally stirred, invited us to sit, and asked us what we had heard and seen. A lively conversation ensued about the nature and texture of prairies, about their peculiar appeal to the human imagination, about how prairies are organized. Not once did the talk turn toward any obscure point of taxonomy. We had been invited not merely to examine that prairie, as if it were a patient, but to embrace it.

So, climb the hill, taking all the time you need. You will find yourself

Prairie Coteau Scientific and Natural Area: blooming wood-lily

eventually on something of a mountaintop with a fine, expansive view of rolling, green hills and a valley full of flowers. Perhaps you will spot a hawk riding a thermal or cruising the ridge of the valley. Somewhere a meadowlark might be singing. You might watch the cotton-ball clouds of summer drifting overhead, casting the hills in patterns of sunshine and shade.

These ridges are gravelly and dry, and their slopes are steep. The grasses, under such conditions, never grow very tall. The walking is easy, and one of the things Nicollet appreciated about the Coteau was that there, even in high summer, the dense swarms of mosquitoes that plagued him in the lowland tall-grass prairies seemed to have disappeared.

Walk until you come to a prospect that pleases you, and then settle in. Instead of going to the prairie, let it come to you. "To carry yourself forward and experience myriad things is delusion," the Zen master Dogan said. "But myriad things coming forth and experiencing themselves is awakening."

As often as you do this, something new will command your attention. The prairie is remarkable for its changeability. From day to day and from week to week, it transforms itself, bearing a new cloak of colors. On a cloudy July day when I visited the Coteau with a friend, it was the brilliant array of wood-lilies, *Lilium philadelphicum,* more common in the northern woods but also present on these dry prairies, that caught our eyes.

The wood-lily is a rather stout species, growing on a sturdy stalk a foot or two high, its intensely green leaves whorled near the top. Its cup-shaped flower, two or three inches across, opens at the pinnacle of the stem, and ranges in hue from vibrant orange to a deep and nearly pure red. Inside the cup, at the base of the petals, there is a random ring of royal purple dots.

Wood-lilies are standoffish, growing not in clusters, like so many prairie plants, but as a widely scattered population of individuals, with no need for numbers to make a splash. A few dozen wood-lilies marching across a hillside give the impression of hundreds or thousands.

My companion did not recognize these lilies by their scientific name, so she decided to give them one of her own. *Welcome back,* she called them. "Welcome back can be a greeting to the grasses, plants, bison, and other wildlife that fled a century ago," she said. "It will also greet city dwellers, who can enjoy being reminded of where they're from. Or, for those who believe in heaven, where they're going. And, for cheerful agnostics, a reminder of where we are."

Prairies have that effect. They seem to provoke something vestigial in our imaginations. Before you know it, on a prairie, bedazzled by the allure of some lily, your mind has run to the state of human souls, or to your place in the universal order.

Catlin's Coteau

This wonderful anomaly in nature . . . is undoubtedly the noblest mound of its kind in the world . . . affording the traveller . . . the most unbounded and sublime views of—nothing at all,—save the blue and boundless ocean of prairies that lie beneath and all around him, vanishing into azure in the distance, without a speck or spot to break their softness.

—George Catlin

Thus Pennsylvania-born artist and ethnographer George Catlin described the Prairie Coteau in a letter to Boston mineralogist Charles T. Jackson. Jackson gave the name *catlinite* to the mineral that Catlin had collected on his eight-month, 2,400-mile journey from New York City to the Prairie Coteau's pipestone quarry. The first European American to set foot in the sacred Indian site had made the journey in 1836 essentially alone, without government backing.

Catlin set out to document, in paintings and journals, the dress, bearing, rituals, and everyday practices of the Indian tribes whose demise, he believed, was imminent. "Nothing short of the loss of my life, shall prevent me from visiting their country and becoming their historian," he wrote, with characteristic fervor. After eight years of travel throughout the West, Catlin had produced 445 paintings and thousands of pencil sketches, and amassed a collection of Indian artifacts that would later fascinate audiences in Philadelphia, London, and Paris.

At the time, Catlin's art was appreciated mostly for its accurate and detailed depiction of the Indians and their customs. More recently, he has been praised for his ability to capture the psychological and spiritual essence of the prairie. His art and journals recorded the many moods the prairie provoked, from despair to fear to ecstasy: "The pedestrian over such a discouraging sea of green, without a landmark before or behind him . . . feels weak and overcome when night falls."

Though Catlin struggled to convince the U.S. Congress to purchase his "Indian gallery," he died penniless in 1872 without achieving that aim. Today, much of his work is displayed at the Smithsonian Institution's National Museum of American Art and the National Gallery of Art, both in Washington, D.C.

Gneiss Outcrops Scientific and Natural Area: water-grooved gneiss formation

A World within a World

From a slight rise in a pasture, the scenery is pastoral: a farmyard to the right; fenced grasslands, piles of field stones, and croplands to the left; behind, the wooded rim of a valley; ahead, an airy river-bottom forest. High in the crook of a big old oak, a raccoon sleeps away the day.

And then, coming up a draw, I suddenly find myself at the edge of a narrow, sparkling lake, contained between parallel cliffs of stone some fifty feet high. I grew up scarcely twenty miles from this place. I never dreamed that such a landscape as this, a canoe country scene, existed within reach of my prairie bluff house. The place is Gneiss Outcrops SNA in the Minnesota River Valley near Granite Falls.

Gneiss—it sounds like *nice*—is the oldest stuff in Minnesota, a rock formed about 3.6 billion years ago out of even older rock.

Gneisses are metamorphic; they began as something else. Those in the Minnesota River Valley started as sedimentary and volcanic rocks that were cooked, folded, injected, and pressed down, over and over again, until they took their present, distinctively banded form—parallel slabs of pink and red rock (granitic gneiss), gray to black ones (hornblende-pyroxene gneiss), and dark gray ones (garnet-biotite gneiss), like landscape-sized slices of layer cake. Nothing seems more immutable than rock, and yet even it bears news of violent and ceaseless change over the vastness of geologic time.

The Minnesota River Valley itself is, in the vicinity of Granite Falls, a couple of miles wide and one hundred feet deep; elsewhere it reaches as much as five miles wide and 250 feet deep, a dramatic gouge in the otherwise flat or gently rolling landscape of central and western Minnesota. The Minnesota River, compared with its valley, is a diminutive flowage, circling now west, now south, now east, now north around the gneiss outcrops within the confines of its towering banks, like some small creature pacing in a giant cage. The Minnesota did not carve the valley; it wanders in the cavernous footprint of its precursor, the River Warren, which drained Glacial Lake Agassiz some nine thousand to eleven thousand years ago. (Warren was Gen. G. K. Warren, an army engineer who first described the origin of the valley.)

Geologists, in their rich nomenclature, call the Minnesota an *underfit* river.

The present-day river is placid and gentle. The two modest drops at Granite Falls, where flocks of white pelicans gather in the springtime, are the only falls in the river's 355-mile course. But the older Warren was, intermittently, a raging and icy torrent. Its power is still written in the gneiss outcrops that resisted it.

These rocky ridges were grassy and nearly treeless 150 years ago when unsuppressed fires still shaped the landscape. Now the climb to the top of them is like a climb, in miniature, up a mountainside through a succession of habitats—hardwood forest at the bottom, shaded, mossy, and be-ferned; then thickets of red cedar, nearly impenetrable in their prickly density; then, on the declivities of the severe summit, blisteringly hot in summer, frigid in the winter winds, prairie grasses and flowers; and finally, along the exposed western edge of the northern outcrop, where the prevailing north-westerlies are felt at their fullest force, a silvery patch of reindeer moss, nestled among rock and pussy-toes, just as on any outcrop in the forests of northeastern Minnesota.

The stone is, in many places, gouged with a lacework of channels and rivulets. These are the tracks, lingering in the stone, of the same turbulent Warren waters that carved the whole valley. Here and there I also find bowl-

Gneiss Outcrops Scientific and Natural Area: plains prickly pear

shaped or post-hole-shaped depressions in the rock, the deepest of them holding puddles of stagnant rainwater and luxuriant growths of algae. Geologists call these potholes. They were made by pebbles that caught and spun in place in the swirling currents of the old river until they ground themselves to sediment in ancient rock.

Among the distinctive flora of these outcrops are two species of cactus. One is the plains prickly pear, whose spectacular flowers are the essence of yellowness and whose maroon fruits are almost as sweet as jam. The other is the brittle cactus (or little prickly pear), which will grab hold of your shoes or pant legs and come along for the ride should you fail to notice it. Three tiny and retiring plants prosper along the edges of ephemeral rock pools: Carolina foxtail, little barley, and mousetail.

Although it has not been seen here, the five-lined skink might live in these outcrops. It does occur nearby on the Blue Devil Valley SNA, another gneiss outcrop site that has not been so extensively invaded by red cedar. The five-lined skink is a small, insect-eating lizard whose bright blue tail (a feature it shares with the more common prairie skink) gives it the common name, blue devil. It is common elsewhere in the eastern United States but is known to occur in Minnesota only in the upper Minnesota River Valley and the limestone outcrops of southeastern Fillmore County and central Houston County.

The narrow lake nestled between the outcrops is probably spring fed. Because it has no inlet, it lies wholly within a watershed visible from its cliff-bound shores, isolated from the runoff pollutants that challenge the vitality of the adjacent river. It is—rare in agricultural Minnesota—a lake whose waters really are sky blue.

As I sat on a ledge above the lake one late spring day, watching the shadows of evening gather and basking in the improbable serenity of the place, a world within a world, an ancient snapping turtle—looking dinosaurian in its craggy carapace—swam into view. It paused below me, stretched its long neck until its snout pierced the surface of the lake, and took a deep, silent breath. The turtle swam on and out of view at a regal pace. A slight evening breeze rippled the waters in its delicate wake. In the distance a small engine roared to life and I started, as if I had drifted off in one century and awakened in the next.

Why Love a Rock?

A mere 1.4 billion years after the birth of the solar system, including Earth—after 900 million years of meteor bombardment of the planet—long before the first dinosaurs trod heavily over the land—before even the simplest one-celled organisms had gathered themselves into an efficiently working unit—granite rocks from the earliest known continental crust were subjected to intense heat and pressure generated far beneath Earth's surface. These rocks metamorphosed into the 3- to 3.6-billion-year-old gneisses we can view today at Gneiss Outcrops SNA.

Amazingly, these rocks remained intact through a subsequent 2.6 billion years of explosive volcanism and massive earthquakes that built mountains, split continents, and folded tons of rock as neatly as paper.

The gneisses persisted unchanged through Minnesota's first tropical age between 450 million and 500 million years ago, when the piece of crust Minnesotans live on today lay near the equator. The rocks survived the shallow Paleozoic seas that advanced and retreated, inundating continents and depositing deep, fossil-laden sediments. They survived the cracking up of the last known supercontinent, Pangaea, and the drift of North America to its present position on the globe. While many rocks throughout North America were weathering into deep, soft, clay-rich soils during a second tropical period 66 million years ago, these gneiss outcrops escaped unchanged.

When the ice age began 2 million years ago, these gneisses suffered the fate of more than 99 percent of Minnesota's bedrock: They were buried under tons of debris left by retreating glaciers. About 10,000 years ago, when the glaciers retreated for the last time, modern humans might have witnessed the torrential Glacial River Warren as it carved out what is now the Minnesota River Valley. The scouring river waters dug through layer upon layer of sand and gravel to expose the gneiss intact—more than 3 billion years after its formation—to our wonderment.

That's why you have to love these rocks.

Felton Prairie Scientific and Natural Area: blooming sunflowers and blazing stars

Subterranean Prairie

I arrived at Felton Prairie SNA, a 410-acre preserve in northwestern Minnesota's Clay County, on a brilliantly sunlit August day and immediately felt disoriented. A prairie is the most deceptive of landscapes. Its geometry is relentlessly horizontal, two-thirds of it filled in fair weather by a faintly blue and trackless sky. A prairie landscape offers no obvious point of reference, nothing for the wandering eye to seize upon as a starting point. As a result, a prairie at first impresses you as empty, featureless, barren.

Overwhelmed by this impression, O. E. Rolvaag asserted in his novel *Giants in the Earth,* the great literary evocation of the prairie landscape, that the unplowed prairie was utterly soundless. While this could not have been literally so, it has the ring of poetic truth. Even the mighty bison of the prairies grunts softly like a pig.

A prairie, for all of its openness, is in many ways a subterranean community. I once heard it likened to a forest in which the canopy opens underground. Indeed, the greater part of the biomass of a prairie is tied up in its massive, deep, and labyrinthine network of roots. There in the sod or just beneath it, most prairie mammals are found.

Blanketed with grasses and forbs, the surface of a prairie looks flat. In the aftermath of a fire, it is revealed to be honeycombed with mounds thrown up by its burrowing creatures, as thoroughly worked as if it had been plowed. Even the prairie's diminutive burrowing owl nests underground.

While I was wandering aimlessly, searching for a way into Felton Prairie SNA, Richard Pemble, a biologist at Moorhead State University, happened by. Several permanent research quadrats have been established on the preserve, and he had come, he explained, to census the plants in them.

"Hop into the car," he said. "I'll show you where to begin."

A few minutes later, he stopped to let me out at the highest point on the prairie, a place where three aspects of its past visibly converge. There was, for one thing, a truck-sized granite boulder, shaped like a mountain in miniature, which was carried down out of the north by one of the glaciers that scoured this landscape during the last ice age. There was the wave-shaped swell on which the rock was perched, one of several fossil shorelines of Glacial Lake

Agassiz, which was formed by an ice dam as the glacial ice began to melt. Agassiz lasted for two thousand years, at its maximum extent burying what is now Felton Prairie in fifty feet of water. And there was the depression in the earth around the rock, trampled out by the generations of bison that used it as a rubbing stone, a place to satisfy their itches.

With the buffalo rock to steer by, I set out across the prairie anew, pausing here to admire an ivory-colored leafhopper, there for a closer look at the delicate flowers of a lobelia, the palest hue of blue. I saw yellow sunflowers, goldenrods, and cinquefoils; white daisy-fleabanes and northern bedstraws; the blue flowers of wild lettuce and harebells; the gray leaves of leadplants and sages; the glistening leaves of the silverleaf scurf-pea; the bronzes of the ripening grasses; the shocking purples of the elegant Flodman's thistle and the blazing stars. Felton Prairie in full bloom at mid-August is the equal, to my eye, of a high mountain meadow.

I circled in every direction from the buffalo rock, my mood growing merrier with each new vista. When I got around to the quadrat that Pemble was surveying, I found him in a merry mood too. He pointed out the grape-fern that he had just spotted. The tiny, feathery fern grows in dry places in the shade of the comparatively towering grasses. Pemble said seventy plant species grow in that one twenty-meter-square plot.

Felton Prairie Scientific and Natural Area: buffalo rock after a prairie burn in spring

When I got back to the buffalo rock, I encountered a delegation of natural resource managers from Ohio, also in high spirits. Eager to get a first-hand look at plants they knew only from books, the botanists in the group dashed, almost like children at an amusement park, from one natural attraction to the next.

"A walk on a prairie always puts me in a good mood," I said to one of them.

"Well, of course," he replied. "The diversity of a place like this is simply intoxicating."

I wandered until long after the other visitors had left. I was finally surprised to realize that I was hungry, parched, and badly sunburned. I went off in search of something to eat.

At sunset I returned to the prairie for one last look around. The day's work had ended in the gravel pits that ring the preserve, and the trucks had stopped running. It was almost preternaturally quiet, except for the lowing of cattle a mile away. From my vantage near the buffalo rock, I could see the land north and west for many miles—the quilt work of farm country, which has its own beauty, a mosaic of green sugar beet fields, yellow sunflower fields, golden patches of small grains, swatches of gray-green grass.

On the horizon, along a country road, a pickup truck passed, too distant to be heard, visible as a pair of lights with a tail of dust rising into the air like a cloud of smoke, brilliantly backlit by the long rays of the setting sun. In the east the moon had already risen and hung in the still-blue sky. Pewter colored and luminescent, the moon looked as if it were a glass globe lit from within, big enough and close enough so that you might leap up and touch it.

Perched on the tall stem of a purple coneflower, a grasshopper sparrow sang its thin, buzzing song. From the thick grass arose a chorus of crickets, as evocative of quiet summer evenings in the American heartland as the sound of surf pounding is of the sea.

In the deep shadows of the last light, the air was already noticeably cooler. A slight breeze swept like a caress across my sunburned brow.

Just at dusk a swarm of mosquitoes arose from the grass and circled my head. The sound of their wings sawing air made a nasty snarl, but only a few of them, mercifully, were in the mood for dinner. A hatch of mayflies, looking ghostly in the crosslight of the setting sun and the rising moon, made their brief acquaintance with the world. Here and there a moth lit upon a flower to take nourishment under the protective cover of dusk. Swallows and dragonflies swept past, making a feast of the gathering insects.

The sky turned mauve and rosy at the horizon as I followed my long shadow across the prairie, which took on a golden glow in the last low sunbeams. The blue of the sky deepened to cobalt and then turned gray. The plants lost their color and turned gray too, then vanished into the shadows. The keening of a mourning dove in the distance and the lowing of the cattle in their pasture brought down the day. Overhead, the first stars began to flicker. With the fall of night, the cloud of mosquitoes hovering above me dissipated. In the gentle light of the full moon, the gray leaves of the sages and the leadplants shone like silver.

It was so utterly peaceful then that I thought of a body of still water, that most tranquil of all natural landscapes. It was the kind of light and the kind of silence that deep-water divers know. Glacial Lake Agassiz, from the unriled depths of which this great flatness emerged, seemed, for a brief moment, to have risen again, to be lapping against its ancient shoreline once more, and I had the sensation of being submerged in it. I stood for a long time, bathed in the watery light of the moon.

Then I got into my car, started the engine, and not bothering to turn on the headlights, drove slowly away.

Felton Prairie Scientific and Natural Area: pocket gopher mounds, evidence of one burrowing species

A Prairie without Ants?

Worldwide, the number of individual ants exceeds the numbers of mammals, birds, reptiles, and amphibians combined, writes myrmecologist (ant scientist) Edward O. Wilson. The world's eighty-eight hundred known ant species do everything from farming fungi and tending other insects as "livestock," to kidnapping slaves and carrying out suicide missions to save their queens.

Ants of the genus *Formica* are earthmovers of the highest order. In the prairie ecosystem, species such as *F. obscuripes* and *F. montana* build dirt mounds averaging two feet tall by two feet wide, sometimes as much as six feet wide. These mounds, "thatched" with sticks and other vegetation, provide quarters for workers as well as chambers for pupae and larvae. The mounds protect the nest from floods and fire and keep the internal temperature and moisture levels relatively constant.

In the Minnesota prairie ecosystem—devoid of native earthworms—this mound-building and tunneling provides an essential service: soil aeration. Aeration facilitates the drainage of rainwater, the exchange of gases by root hairs, and the infiltration of gases necessary for decomposition of dead plants and animals.

Mounds serve other functions as well. "Trash heaps" of discarded plant and animal material inside the mound concentrate nutrients that support a lush growth of plants on abandoned nests. The same trash heaps make substrates for the sprouting of seeds that ants have collected, partially eaten, and discarded.

Another ant behavior might affect the diversity and abundance of prairie plant species. Some ants tend aphids, which suck sap from the roots, stems, and leaves of plants such as sunflowers, aspen, and dogwood. The aphids extrude a honeydew that the ants feed on, and the ants in turn protect the aphids from other insects. The host plant, in some cases, appears to benefit from the elimination of leaf-eating insects, producing taller stems and more seeds.

Some ants share their mounds with other insects such as scarab beetles. The ants do cemetery duty by clearing the ground of 90 percent of small animal corpses.

Most myrmecologists would have to agree: You can't have a prairie without the ants.

Black Lake Bog Scientific and Natural Area: peatlands and forest

Luminaries of the Bog

The water in Black Lake is not actually black; it is more nearly the color of well-aged leather. The lake's color derives, in fact, from tannin, which concentrates in the leaves of plants deprived of nitrogen. Black Lake is a bog lake, and bogs are poor in minerals and rich in inhospitable qualities: acidity, the perpetual chill that lingers in them, the scarcity of dry land. Mosquitoes figure prominently on the short list of creatures that adore bogs.

The lake, now jointly preserved by Minnesota and Wisconsin as Black Lake Bog SNA—our only multistate SNA—is not the sort of place you would ever just happen upon, although it is only a couple of hours north of the Twin Cities. You drive east from Sandstone on paved county roads, then north again on gravel, through the ghost town of Belden. When the road ends altogether, you park your car and proceed on foot for another mile and a half along an

Black Lake Bog Scientific and Natural Area: bull moose

abandoned railroad grade until you reach the Black River. There you put in the canoe you've carried with you and paddle downstream, navigating carefully lest you get diverted into a side channel and find yourself hung up precariously on a beaver dam. In a mile or so, you reach the lake, its shallow broody center giving way to floating masses of lilies and pondweeds and these to open bog or spruce and tamarack swamp.

A pack of wolves occasionally crosses this country, and now and then a moose, or perhaps a black bear seeking a place to den up for the winter. When I visited, three or four blinds—weekend dwellings for the few waterfowl hunters who had found their way into the bog during the fall migration—perched like fortifications along the shore of the lake. No longer allowed since the land became an SNA, the blinds were soon to be torn down. The one I inspected had two tiny compartments—one for shooting, the other a windowless bunker as tight as a ship's quarters—and a boardwalk leading to a privy as tiny as the blind, tucked discreetly into a clump of willows. A trapper might sometimes venture into this country in season too; fishers, martens, beavers, and bobcats live in the neighborhood.

Between 1911 and the mid-1930s, a modest bustle of human activity was a regular feature of the Black Lake area. The railroad was running then, and nearby there were lumber camps and plants that turned out lumber, veneer, barrel staves, cedar shakes, toothpicks, and railroad ties. But the supply of harvestable timber was soon exhausted, and in the mid-1930s a fire swept through, bringing human occupation of the region to an end.

On the late September day I spent there, a deeper silence reigned than I can remember hearing in any remote wilderness. The migratory songbirds had already headed south, the geese had not yet arrived, and not so much as a crow or an airplane passed overhead to break the stillness. The loudest sound was that of the lily pads lifting in the breeze and falling back again onto the surface of the lake.

It was, despite the abnormal silence, a beguiling place in bugless September. Bright sunlight sparkled on the dark water, a bank of storm clouds gathered dramatically on the horizon, and between the two, the brilliant yellows of aspens and tamaracks and the scarlet leaves of scattered maples made a vivid show of autumn.

My companions—Bob Djupstrom, supervisor of the SNA Program, and SNA management assistant Tim Marion—and I beached our canoe and set out across the bog on foot. Traversing the plush pile carpet of sphagnum mosses—plants capable of absorbing twenty-five times their weight in water—was like hiking in knee-deep marshmallows, the ultimate aerobic exercise. Djupstrom carried a topographic map and a compass in his day pack, and as we walked, he bent tamarack and spruce twigs to mark our trail.

The reason for these precautions soon became apparent. A bog is one of the flattest places on earth. Although peatlands from the air have such a distinctive topography that they are sometimes called patterned peatlands, from the ground the terrain seems featureless. One tamarack or stunted spruce or hummock of sphagnum looks remarkably like the next. It would be easy to wander absent-mindedly a few hundred yards into this landscape and to find yourself utterly disoriented.

We headed toward one of the few contours on the topographic map, an island of northern hardwoods that had found purchase on a ten-foot rise in the landscape. But before we got to that high ground—to the place where ferns grew in firm earth, and the trunks of fallen trees moldered into dust, and pale dry birch leaves lay scattered in the dark woods like stars—we paused to taste the bitter cranberries, still pale as roses. It was then that we noticed the round-leaved sundews.

There are, if you happen to care about such things, plants you want to meet in the same way that there are people from history you would love, some evening, to entertain at dinner. I had been wanting such an introduction to the sundews, which captured the imagination of no less a naturalist than Charles Darwin. After Darwin finished his revolutionary work on evolution, he took up the subject of carnivorous plants, publishing a still-standard volume on them, paying particular attention to the sundews, which he was the first to recognize as carnivores.

Black Lake Bog Scientific and Natural Area: round-leaved sundews

His fascination with *Drosera,* the scientific name for sundews, ran in the family. Darwin's grandfather wrote a famous (and somewhat erotic) poem about them, and his son conducted experiments that established beyond doubt that sundews are insect-eaters.

"I care more about the *Drosera,*" Darwin wrote, "than the origin of all the species in the world."

The species of sundew that grows at Black Lake Bog, *D. rotundifolia,* is one Darwin knew; it occurs around the globe in the northern hemisphere. It is a plant of modest proportions, a rosette of tiny, round leaves, each on a slender stalk, hiding within the sphagnum.

The leaves are covered with purple hairs, longer at the edges than at the center. Each of these hairs bears a clear droplet that sparkles in the sun. The fancy of the common name, which is at least as old as the first medieval illustrations of the plant, was that these droplets were bits of dew, caught charmingly by a pretty little plant. Darwin's grandfather, in his poem, saw the plant as a slender-waisted little queen garbed in royal silk.

In fact the droplets are bits of glue, stickier than honey. An unfortunate insect lights on one of the leaves, finds itself caught by a leg or two, thrashes about to break free, and with every motion brushes up against another hair, getting itself all the more firmly stuck. These struggles, perhaps by setting off electrical impulses within the plant, prompt it to curl up the leaf, in which the hapless insect is soon entombed. Then the plant exudes enzymes that digest the prey and allow it to be absorbed. When the sundew has consumed its victim, the leaf opens, the empty shell of the insect wafts away in a breeze, new droplets of glue are exuded through the ends of the hairs, and the sparkling table is set again for the next meal.

Sundews have tuberous roots and are capable of photosynthesis, but they do not prosper when they are deprived of their insect diet. We do not credit plants with ingenuity, or even with behavior, which is why it angered some critics of Darwin, ahead of his time as usual, that he should attribute carnivorousness to mere vegetation. But it can be said with impunity that Nature is ingenious, and that the sundews are one instance of this, a splendid adaptation to life in a place where the soil is poor, minerals are scarce, and insects are bountiful.

The *Drosera,* it might even be said with a certain amount of humility, have found a way to thrive in an environment too extreme to support human life. No wonder Darwin, who made adaptation into a theory of life, admired them above all other plants.

Sweet Sphagnum

You wouldn't think a lowly moss could hold up a whole world. But sphagnum enables a host of bog-forest species to grow over cold, stagnant water. In addition, the moss serves practical purposes for humans and preserves artifacts of our vegetational, climatic, and cultural past.

A microscopic view of the moss reveals large, dead, porous cells interspersed with smaller, photosynthetic ones. The large cells absorb water up to twenty times the moss's weight, as well as gases that keep the moss buoyant.

When sphagnum cells die, they release tannins and acids, which inhibit the growth of decomposing bacteria. As a result, dead sphagnum (or peat) accumulates at a rate of two to five inches per century. The thickening mat forms a healthy substrate for spruce and tamarack seeds, which would otherwise fail to germinate in the acidic bog water. The mat, stabilized somewhat by interlocking tree roots, also supports heath family species such as bog-laurel and leather-leaf, whose fleshy leaves are adapted to retain moisture from air and rain-water since the plants cannot use the acidic bog water. The tops of sphagnum hummocks provide prime real estate for species such as the pitcher-plant, which grows as far away from the acidic water as possible.

Sphagnum peatlands store tremendous amounts of carbon. When burned, two tons of peat release as much energy as two tons of firewood or one ton of coal.

Sphagnum, with its phenomenal absorbency, has lined the diapers of American Indian infants and dressed the wounds of soldiers. Modern gardeners add "peat moss," dried sphagnum, to soil to hold water, absorb nutrients, and retard the growth of fungi and bacteria.

Perhaps most intriguing of all, the cold, sterile environment of sphagnum preserves the outer shells of pollen grains, enabling scientists to identify the types and abundance of plant species present over time. And it prevents decay of bodies such as the two-thousand-year-old remains of humans found in bogs in northern Europe. Such well-preserved specimens give clues to species and ways of life that have all but disappeared.

Lost Lake Peatland Scientific and Natural Area: tamarack and spruce bog

A Waterlogged Desert

My favorite natural communities, like my favorite people, are those that persist and flourish despite powerful disadvantages. Among Minnesota's natural communities, the northern peatlands are the most compelling example of the type. The landscape of the peatlands is composed of rock and water. The water is stagnant and short of oxygen, and the rock, where it is covered at all, carries a parsimonious mantle of soil.

Winters in this country are long and fiercely frigid; the air temperature in the dead of winter sometimes drops to fifty degrees below zero. Even when the temperature rises to one hundred degrees in midsummer, the dark recesses of the waterlogged peat resist warming. As late as July, the roots of bog plants may still be partially frozen. Organic matter in this sodden and frosty environment decomposes so slowly that the whole landscape is impoverished of nutrients.

Despite this inhospitable environment, a distinctive community of plants and animals has conspired to exist, limited in the number of its species, but long on genetic ingenuity.

Minnesota has more than six million acres of peatlands, the richest assemblage in the lower forty-eight. Remote and difficult to penetrate, they remain largely unspoiled. They constitute the state's last wilderness frontier. In 1991 the Legislature protected eighteen of these peatlands, the best examples of the various forms they can take in Minnesota. One of them, the Lost Lake Peatland, lies a few miles south of Lake Vermilion in St. Louis County.

I visited Lost Lake Peatland one snowy December morning in the company of Marshall Helmberger, who publishes a local newspaper called the *Timberjay.* Helmberger, a peatlands enthusiast, makes his home on a rocky ridge overlooking the swamp. The core of the peatland has been designated an SNA, but because the county owns the rest of the peatland, it remains substantially unprotected.

It was about ten degrees and a light snow was falling, driven on the steady northerly of an advancing cold front, as we set out on skis across Lost Lake. The lake, about a square mile, has the shape of a teardrop, also the typical shape of the islands of trees in peatlands. To the west, a line of low hills, the extension of a long rock ridge through the swamp, rose against the horizon. To the east, two prominent headlands of rock pressed against the shoreline. In the lee of one of them, a lone man huddled on the ice beside a snowmobile, fishing. Man and machine both, in the expanse of trackless snow and ice, looked toy sized.

We glided across the ice, the sound of our skis muffled in the wind. Though hardly more than a mile from the end of a road, we were venturing into a world seldom visited by humans and about which a great many scientific mysteries remain.

On the northern shore, we paused to remove our skis. There had been relatively little snow; we would go up the ridge and into the swamp on foot. Out of the wind, it was mild and silent, as if we had stepped indoors out of a storm. Animal tracks traced the shoreline, giving way in fifty yards to the long belly troughs that told us the creature was another skier of sorts, an otter.

We climbed the ridge through a forest of conifers and hardwoods. Atop the ridge, many red maple saplings dangled broken limbs and trunks, which had been doubled back at a height of five or six feet and snapped but not severed. These were signs, Helmberger said, of browsing moose.

Then we came upon the skull of a buck deer with a fine rack, cleanly stripped of its hair, hide, and flesh. The head had been neatly severed at the neck. We could find no other traces of the animal. It was impossible to say how the

Lost Lake Peatland Scientific and Natural Area: otter tracks, black-backed three-toed woodpecker

deer had met its demise, but this is, Helmberger noted, timber wolf country.

"This is bear country too?" I asked.

Absolutely, Helmberger said, but during the summer the bears tend to avoid the bogs, as most large animals do, sticking to the higher ground along the edges of the swamp. "In fact," he said, "it turns out that the ridge where we built our house is on a migratory route for bears, so we see them all summer long." In the winter, however, the animals, especially male bears, hibernate in forested bogs, sometimes not even bothering to dig a den.

We ascended the promontory for a view into the heart of the swamp, vast and mostly flat, covered in low, brown-leaved shrubs and studded with spindly black spruces, stretching away from the lake to the horizon. Helmberger, who has been exploring this swamp for more than a decade, had thought, as we left his house, to tuck a compass into his pocket. "It's pretty easy to get lost out there," he said.

We turned away from the view and spotted a black-backed three-toed woodpecker. It was working the trunk of a spruce twenty feet from where we stood. It was indifferent to our presence, too unaccustomed, perhaps, to disturbance to be wary. The word "black" hardly does justice to the velveteen darkness of the bird's back feathers. This woodpecker is a specialist in bark-boring insects, which it uncovers not by hammering away at the wood but by prying loose flakes of bark and flipping them away with a sidewise thrust of its bill.

We left the woodpecker to its work and went down the north face of the ridge, crossing the trail of a fisher, a weasel-like creature identifiable by the five toes of its tracks.

The swamp here was strikingly different from the one we had seen to the south. There were cattails, irises, bog birches, alders, and tamaracks, which shed their needles in winter. The vegetation rising above the sphagnum moss was more grassy than shrubby. This was a sedge fen, Helmberger said, where the swamp probably benefited from a slightly richer supply of nutrients, carried down the ridge in runoff.

The sedge fen, made up of an intricate pattern of moss hummocks and pools, proved treacherous going. The ice on the pools, thin because the water was in motion, gave way without warning. We did a slow, awkward dance across the fen, testing the way ahead with our heels, leaping from hummock to hummock, grasping at tall shrubs and gangly tamaracks for support.

These peatlands appear from the air so distinctly textured that biologists refer to them as patterned peatlands. The fen we were crossing was a ribbed fen with alternating narrow bands of peat, called *strings,* and slender pools of water, called *flarks.* Another kind of fen, which does not have this ribbing, is called a *featureless water track.*

We were headed, I was about to discover, from the fen, by way of an island, into a bog. Bogs are formed in pools of surface water; fens in places where there is an upwelling of groundwater. Because of the differences in hydrology, bogs and fens have different water chemistry and composition of plant species. Bogs are acidic; relatively nutrient-rich fens are more alkaline.

Biologists have also divided bog landforms into two types: raised and crested raised. Lost Lake has both kinds of fens and bogs, but the site has been protected for the high quality of its raised bogs, ranked ten on a scale of ten by the scientific committee that surveyed Minnesota's peatlands in the late 1980s.

Once we had reached the island, we found ourselves immersed in a dense balsam fir grove. When we broke out into the sunlight again, we entered the raised bog. Above the snow, in landscape as flat as a football field, rose the dark trunks of black spruces, widely spaced, the tallest of them less than twenty feet high.

"Don't be deceived by the size of these trees," Helmberger said. "They may well be one hundred years old, or more. In this environment, they may grow an inch a year or less."

Several feet of a trunk could be submerged below the bog's surface, Helmberger said. While most landscapes erode over time, a bog rises. It begins as a floating mass of vegetation, which accumulates and deepens until the

Lost Lake Peatland Scientific and Natural Area: bog-laurel in late spring

whole quivering mass eventually becomes grounded. The vegetation continues to pile up, subsuming stationary objects such as trees. Spruces cope by cloning themselves. They send out roots from their lowest branches. When the bog rises to meet the branches, new saplings emerge from them.

Surveying the spruces, we stood in a knee-high thicket of shrubs. Helmberger pointed out the most common shrubs: Labrador-tea, bog-laurel, bog-rosemary, and leather-leaf, all members of the heath family. Then he pointed out something so obvious that I had not noticed it, that they all still had their leaves. There are so few nutrients in this ecosystem—those that are available come in the form of dust, rain, and minute ground seepage—that few bog plants can afford the expense of manufacturing new leaves every spring, Helmberger explained. This frugality gives the plants another advantage in a short growing season: They are prepared to begin the work of photosynthesis the instant it becomes possible.

We examined the leaves. They were narrow, thick, leathery, with a tendency to curl—all traits you find in the leaves of desert plants, said Helmberger. Although a bog is an ecosystem built upon water, the roots of these plants are sealed in frost and ice for much of the year and cannot take up water. Like desert plants, bog plants live in constant danger of dehydrating.

A landscape that rises rather than erodes, the surface of which trembles like a trampoline, in a climate so severe that the plants are evergreen, a water-logged desert—the perfect demonstration, I thought, as we laboriously made our way back toward the lake, sinking with every step into the frozen but insubstantial sphagnum moss, that truth is often stranger than fiction.

Along the way, we paused at the dried flower stalk of a pitcher-plant. Pitcher-plants, sundews, and bladderworts are all bog plants that have devised strategies, in this hungry environment, for capturing, liquefying, and consuming insects. It is a world in which the plants feed upon the insects, and not the other way around.

But we did not linger to contemplate this strange turn of the tables. We were near ice again, something solid, and when we reached it, we strapped on our skis and set out, with a wind so strong at our backs that we sailed across the scallops of drifting snow, toward a more familiar landscape, gentler and more hospitable, no doubt, but perhaps, for that reason, just a bit duller too.

Strings and Flarks

If the language alone is enough to stymie you, hang in there. You're not the only one who's puzzled. Scientists have been asking for decades what causes the string and flark pattern—parallel strips of vegetation alternating with pools of water—of certain peatlands.

Amid a plethora of possibilities, University of Minnesota researcher Paul Glaser suggests that the ribbed fens typical of north-central and northwestern Minnesota's broad, flat, glacial lake plains might develop as follows:

1. First, sedge lawns form along drainage routes on gently sloped land.
2. Because cold, upwelling groundwater saturates these lawns, dead plants and animals decompose very slowly; a layer of partially decomposed material, called peat, begins to form—at a rate of two to five inches per century.
3. These absorbent peat layers cause the water table, or highest point reached by groundwater, to rise and flood the lower-lying areas of the sedge lawn, thus forming pools.
4. The inundated sedges die off, so peat deposition essentially stops. The peat already on the pool's floor decomposes further and settles, so that the pool bottom deepens.
5. In unflooded areas, peat deposition continues at a normal rate. As the strips of vegetation get higher, the water table rises even more, causing more flooding. Pools get deeper, and the cycle continues, a self-perpetuating feedback loop.

This process does not depend on external factors such as rainfall rates or air temperatures. It depends instead on the height of the water table and the direction of groundwater flow. From the air, the pattern is unmistakable—strings and flarks form perpendicular to the down-slope flow of groundwater. (Pools forming parallel to the groundwater flow would simply break through the vegetation wall and drain into a lower pool.) If workers build ditches to lower the water table, trees invade, and the ribbed pattern eventually disappears.

Pine and Curry Island Scientific and Natural Area: piping plover eggs

One Island Alone

We drove to the end of the road, parked the car at a resort on the south shore of Lake of the Woods, got into a small fishing boat, and headed down a creek toward open water, Steve Maxson at the helm and Katie Haws in the bow with me.

Maxson slipped on a rain jacket, looked at the sky, and shrugged his shoulders. Bad weather comes with the territory.

Maxson is a DNR wildlife researcher specializing in shorebirds. During May, June, and July, he spends two or three days a week in this boat observing, and in some ways mothering, Minnesota's last population of nesting piping plovers.

The plovers reside on the little island where we're headed. A shorebird unique to North America, the piping plover is on the state endangered species list. The federal government lists it as endangered in the Great Lakes region and threatened elsewhere in the United States.

Haws, who manages nongame wildlife programs for the DNR in northwestern Minnesota, was making one of her regular visits to monitor the breeding success of common terns, another species fighting for survival in Minnesota. The terns maintain a large breeding colony on the island, one of only six colonies in Minnesota.

Our route took us past Morris Point, through the channel between the point and a sliver of sand unofficially called Tern Island, and across a broader second channel to Pine and Curry Island, a barrier island off the mouth of the Rainy River that is more than four miles long and only a couple of hundred yards across at its widest point. Morris Point and the island together make up Pine and Curry Island SNA, which has been set aside primarily to protect nesting habitat for piping plovers and common terns.

Barrier islands are inherently mutable places, subject to the relentless rearrangements of ice, wind, and waves. Within the past century, what is now Pine and Curry Island had been a peninsula, then a pair of islands—hence the odd double name—and most recently, the long spit of sand that we were circumnavigating.

Around the turn of the century, the other end of the island was the site of a thriving fishing village, LeClair. For a brief time LeClair had all the characteristics of a village on the make, including dwellings, a store, ice houses, packing plants, a caviar factory, and even—from 1898 until 1902— a post office. By the time an International Boundary Map was published in 1912–13, the village had been damaged by a large storm and abandoned. The land on which it had stood had been washed away and redeposited by the waves.

Lake of the Woods is vast and capable of developing awesome waves. "It can get pretty rough out here," Maxson said in his laconic way, casting a glance at the storm clouds gathering overhead.

Maxson slowed the boat as we approached Morris Point. Piping plovers nest on both sides of the channel, their presence advertised by a grid-work of small steel posts and chartreuse nylon string that guards the sandy beaches. The grids were devised a couple of years ago to screen out ring-billed gulls. The gulls compete for nesting space and prey on the eggs of the smaller plovers, which easily avoid the string. The grids seem to have worked. The gaudy color has apparently contributed to their effectiveness, Maxson said.

He said that four plover chicks were hatched on the point this season, but for the moment they were nowhere to be seen. Plovers can be hard to spot in any case, because they are perfectly camouflaged, "as pallid as a beach flea or sand crab," the Peterson field guide says, "the color of dry sand." As we searched in vain for the chicks, an adult flew overhead and landed in the grass at the head of the beach. To my eyes, it was distinguishable only as a faint, brief blur. "That's the adult male from the nest at the other end of Tern Island," Maxson said, more to himself than

Pine and Curry Scientific and Natural Area: common tern

to his companions. I looked at him in astonishment, but his attention had already been diverted by something else that I could not see and he did not explain.

Maxson opened the throttle a bit, and we entered the lake side of the bay, passing the colony of terns, some four hundred in number, which rose into the air, screaming, circling above the sand like a swarm of enormous white bees. At the western end of the main island, we passed another large flock of birds. These were gulls, mainly Franklin's, which, the bird-tag evidence suggests, nest in Agassiz National Wildlife Refuge, seventy miles southwest. After the young gulls have fledged, some of the adults fly to Pine and Curry Island to loaf and fatten up for a couple of weeks before setting out on the long flight south to their winter grounds. Here gulls are vacationers, like the fishing parties whose boats had begun to dot the waters of the bay.

Up the island the top of a towering white pine supported a bald eagle nest. An adult eagle perched above the nest gave us the proverbial eagle eye, a fierce and regal stare, unassailable. Barely visible over the craggy rim of the enormous nest peeked an eaglet. Haws scrutinized the nest through her binoculars but saw no sign of a second eaglet. Still, she smiled at the sight of one eaglet. This nest, she said, was empty last year.

About a mile farther east along Pine and Curry Island, at a place where the sand rises into full-fledged dunes, Maxson turned the boat toward shore.

When we stepped ashore, we might have been at any one of a thousand classic resort places: a grand sweep of wide, white sand beach; beyond it, blue water curving away to the horizon; the pacific sound of waves lapping sand; and overhead the keening of gulls.

Sand beach communities are as rare in the upper Midwest as the birds that nest in them. Pine and Curry Island is the largest undeveloped sand beach in the region. Above the wave line in the sand, tentacles of beach-pea and thickets of wormwood and sand-cherry had taken root despite the absence of soil. Here and there fronds of Canada wild rye waved. "When the sand-cherries are blooming," Maxson said, "the fragrance will about knock you out of your boat seat."

Maxson led us across a large blowout and pointed to a featureless spot in the sand. "There was a piping plover nest here earlier this season," he said, "here or within two meters of this spot. Not successful."

We headed back toward the beach. Although it is strictly against SNA rules, I wished I could be left alone there for a few days to absorb the full splendor of that remote place. The one jarring note was a faint, slightly sweet stench, like that of rotting flesh, carried on a breeze that quickened as the skies looked ever more menacing.

Maxson pointed out the line of flotsam washed up along the beach, one or two feet wide, two or three inches deep, and stretching out of sight in either direction. "We get tremendous hatches of mayflies here," he said. "There was one a couple of days ago. That's what this material drifted up along the beach is, the bodies of mayflies."

I looked up and down the long beach, wondering how many billions of individuals were represented in this astounding drift of mayfly detritus. I saw why that sparse spit of sand attracts insectivores such as the gulls and plovers in such numbers.

We got into the boat and made the turn around Oak Point at the far end of the island. During the late 1950s, the Sidney Moorhead family owned the island and operated a small bait and food shop on Oak Point. It catered to the summertime fishing traffic on the lake.

Now only the foundations of the Moorhead buildings remain, and the beach at Oak Point is being overtaken by shrubbery, which is being hand-cut to preserve the piping plover nesting site there. Maxson pointed out the adult male plover hovering in the vegetation at the edge of the beach. The males are the primary tenders of the chicks, he said.

It's the rarity of the birds that makes the loss of habitat so critical. "If these were killdeer, we wouldn't think much of it," he said, "but with the piping plovers, there is so little choice." His voice trailed off. Given the threat

Pine and Curry Island Scientific and Natural Area: midges washed ashore

to the species, the DNR has little choice but to try to maintain that habitat.

A decade ago, between twenty and thirty pairs of piping plovers nested on Pine and Curry Island. This year, only six pairs nested and produced seven fledglings. "That's the whole state population," he said.

Maxson revved the engine, and we turned back toward Morris Point. At the tern colony, we beached the boat again so that Haws and Maxson could take census at two chicken-wire enclosures, which were put around the new nests to confine the chicks so that the researchers could measure the reproductive success of the birds.

As we approached the enclosures, the adult terns took to the air, circling a hundred feet overhead and making a din that sounded like the distant roar of a fall afternoon football crowd. Haws and Maxson worked quickly, anxious to disturb the birds as briefly as possible. They climbed into the enclosures and rounded up all of the downy birds, which peeped like barnyard chicks yet hid so effectively beneath the sparse vegetation they were hard to spot even within the small enclosures. To make an accurate count, they put the chicks into a five-gallon bucket, tossing aside the one dead chick they found. They also counted the tan and brown-speckled eggs that remained to be hatched. Then they released the chicks they had rounded up. Within a couple of minutes, we were on the water again.

I asked Haws what accounts for the dead chicks. "We don't always know," she said. "But we can tell when there's been major predation. In 1988 there was a mink here and there were dead chicks strewn all over. This year four hundred terns fledged."

Mink, foxes, skunks, gulls, and great horned owls all prey on the chicks and eggs. The lives of these birds begin in shallow and indefensible depressions in nearly bare sand. It seems miraculous that any of them make it. At Pine and Curry Island, the birds get whatever assistance their human caretakers can offer. The grids of gaudy string fend off the gulls. The nesting sites are posted as wildlife sanctuaries against human visitors who might unwittingly jeopardize the young by their presence. After the mink's killing spree was discovered, the DNR began to trap mammalian predators on the island. Persistent great horned owls have been shot.

Perhaps in part because of these efforts, the island's common tern population has increased in recent years. The same cannot be said for the island's piping plovers, whose numbers have declined steadily since the mid-1980s.

That's what Maxson's long hours of observations from his boat are about. "I watch a pair of plovers for half an hour, recording any interactions with other species and all opportunities to interact. I note who was involved in these interactions and what happened. Then I move on to another pair of plovers and do the same." Maxson is trying to learn from this systematic observation what threats exist to the nesting success of the birds.

One suspect on his list of possible competitors is another, somewhat larger ground-nesting plover, the noisy killdeer. But it takes patience, persistence, and a bit of luck to piece together this kind of story. Often, the dramatic interaction takes place when Maxson is not there. For example, he said, between visits, a male piping plover developed a gimpy leg.

No sooner had Maxson said this than the injured bird put in an appearance at the edge of the beach. It was strikingly handsome, sand-colored above with a snow-white breast and a black neckband. It had yellow legs and a yellow beak with a black tip. As we watched it from the boat, the bird uttered two cries that revealed why it is called the piping plover. The song was simplicity itself, a short *peep-lo,* the first note higher than the second, but flutelike in tone, deeply timbred, clarion, and, despite its brilliance, melancholy.

With the sound ringing in our ears, Maxson throttled the engine to full speed and we bounced our way across the now-choppy bay toward the creek and the dock from which we had launched.

Maxson paused only long enough to allow Haws and me to climb out of the boat; then he set off again, just as rain began to fall. He still had precious hours of daylight and a vigil to keep with the last representatives of one of Minnesota's rarest species of birds.

Pine and Curry Island Scientific and Natural Area: piping plover on nest

Three, but Still Counting

Only three breeding pairs of piping plovers nested in the Lake of the Woods vicinity, including Pine and Curry Island SNA, in 1998. That's down from a high of forty-four pairs in 1984. Scientists have examined these populations continuously since 1982, when University of Minnesota–Duluth researchers began a study of the species' reproductive success. This study, the longest for any one piping plover population, has yielded a few answers and many new questions about what this bird needs to survive.

Found only in North America, the piping plover *(Charadrius melodus)* is one of more than sixty plover species worldwide. Populations along the East Coast and in the Great Lakes region have been all but eliminated due to development and recreational use of the unvegetated sandy beaches the plovers prefer for nesting.

At Pine and Curry Island, loss of habitat and predation are two major factors in the plover's low breeding success, says Katie Haws, DNR nongame wildlife specialist. Waves and wind continually erode the beach where plovers nest.

Meanwhile, the opposite phenomenon—sand deposition—has formed a peninsula that makes the island accessible to mainland predators such as raccoons, foxes, and skunks, as well as humans and dogs, which scare plovers off their nests. Gulls prey on plover chicks and eggs and compete for nesting habitat.

DNR managers are trying to increase the number and success of piping plover nests. They created three sanctuary areas, which are off limits to people during the plover breeding and fledging season from April 15 to September 1. (These sanctuaries also protect the largest Minnesota population of common terns, now threatened in the state.) Wire mesh enclosures with tops of interwoven nylon string are placed around each nest to help prevent access by ground and airborne predators. The tiny plovers walk through the mesh. Workers remove the nests of ring-billed gulls to discourage the gulls from returning to the island; other predators are trapped and removed. Managers also monitor lake levels, and record the number of nests, hatches per nest, and chicks fledged to calculate breeding success for each nesting pair.

Lutsen Scientific and Natural Area: white pine overlooking Poplar River

Tales from Lutsen Woods

I visited Lutsen SNA on a luminous day in early April. The temperature was mild, the air calm, the cloudless sky brilliant blue, the deep snow dusted with flakes that had fallen in the night. The place looked as immaculate as a dinner table set for guests.

The night before, in my motel room, I had been reading a book about the Vienna Woods, the region of low, forested mountains that surrounds the Austrian capital, inspiring artists as various as Beethoven and Franz Kafka. The book began with a line by the poet W.H. Auden, who knew the Vienna Woods well. "A culture is not better than its woods," he wrote.

I imagine that the low mountains of the North Shore bear some resemblance to the Vienna Woods, and Lutsen SNA preserves the best of the highlands: 720 acres of old-growth northern hardwood forests—the most extensive on the North Shore—along two ridges, Eagle Mountain and Raven Ridge, which rise one thousand feet above Lake Superior. The crags offer panoramic views of the lake, the rugged Sawtooth Mountains, and the vast forests extending to the northwest.

Some of the trees at Lutsen—towering white spruces, paper birches, yellow birches, soaring sugar maples—have stood unravaged by fire, wind, or human exploitation for three centuries or more, home to bears and wolves, shady nurseries to spring-blooming wildflowers, nesting places for the richest assemblage of songbirds in Minnesota.

On this day when I set out to encounter these woods, the land was still locked in the embrace of a hard winter. In places forty inches of snow covered the ground. But already my guide, Lloyd Scherer, and I could see signs of impending spring. The snow, dense enough to make the snowshoeing easy, was beginning to melt, and the ravens and the Canada jays were beginning to nest.

We had not gone far when we came upon wolf scat, bristling with deer hair, that had been exposed and dried by the sun. The Lutsen pack has three wolves, Scherer said, probably an alpha pair and one of their offspring, which maintain a rather small territory of about twenty square miles. We walked on several hundred yards and there, as if to affirm Scherer's testimony, were wolf tracks leading out of the woods onto the snowmobile trail that skirts the southern edge of the preserve.

"Let's see," Scherer said. "There were three of them, one here, another following, and this one. They were obviously in no hurry. They were headed, as you can see, in that direction. This is where something caught that one's attention. You can see where it veered off to the left and paused."

Scherer is intimately familiar with the wolves, as he is with every detail of these woods. He first came to them in the early 1950s, a migrant from Pennsylvania. He had learned to love nature in Pennsylvania, but the state had grown too tame for his tastes. In his adopted highlands, he worked at several jobs until he could establish his own nursery, a business that left him free to wander the woods during the long winters. He has wandered far enough to wear out three pairs of snowshoes.

Although he never had much money, Scherer acquired 240 acres of the woods at the heart of what is now Lutsen SNA. Then he gave them to the people of Minnesota. But he is not eager to talk about any of this, and the woods conspicuously do not bear his name. He is a man who loves wild land more than the sound of his own name.

We walked on. I confessed that I had no acquaintance with yellow birches. Scherer's eyebrows lifted.

A few minutes later, he asked, "And what do we have here?"

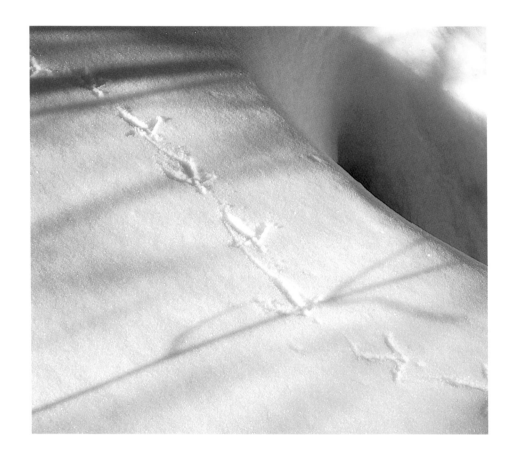

Lutsen Scientific and Natural Area: ruffed grouse tracks

I studied the bird tracks in the snow. "You tell me," I said.

"A chicken!"

"Ah! A grouse," I said. "Spruce?"

"No, no," he said. "There are no spruce grouse here. Ruffed. And what was it up to?"

I studied the tracks again like a dimwitted pupil.

"Well, let's see," Scherer said, as if he had asked the question for his own benefit. "The bird walked over there," he said, pointing to the exposed roots of a toppled tree, "and then it came across to here," pointing to another mass of exposed roots, "and then it walked to here and flew away. I'd say it came to collect grit for its gizzard."

When we next paused, my attention was directed to a tree, obviously a birch, but with bark that had a bronze sheen where the sun struck it. I was ready for him.

"Yellow birch," I said.

"Yellow birch."

He broke a twig from a sapling and handed it to me. "Smell it," he said. When I did, my nostrils were filled with a strong aroma like that of wintergreen, fresh and springlike.

"Yellow birch," Scherer said. "I like to make a tea of it. I whittle some

Lutsen Scientific and Natural Area: paper birch and yellow birch

shavings of the bark and steep them overnight in cold water, and in the morning all I have to do is heat the liquid and I've got a fine tea. Try one of the buds," he said.

I plucked a bud from the twig, chewed it, and the fine flavor of wintergreen tea filled my mouth.

"That's what the tea of the yellow birch tastes like," he said.

We wandered the whole day in that woods through the dazzle of paper birches in snow, the dappled shade of huddled cedars, the soft light falling among dispersed maples and black ash trees. A woodpecker called, a raven floated high overhead with a coarse croak, now and then a chickadee chattered cheerfully, a pair of barred owls hooted to each other. There was a trickle of water in the seepage of a white cedar swamp. But mainly there were the two of us and the light falling among tall trees and the hush of wildness.

We ate our lunches. I sat on the trunk of a downed spruce, Scherer on a bench made of his snowshoes. Then we started up the adjacent slope. We saw the tracks of a coyote, a red-backed vole, a white-footed mouse, a short-tailed shrew, and red squirrels. Unseen by us, a pine marten scampered across the snow and up a tree, leaving behind its trail.

Scherer showed me a balm of Gilead, or balsam poplar, with its deeply grooved bark like that of its cottonwood cousins on the plains, and I thought of my favorite spiritual. He showed me the scarlet twigs of mountain maple. He showed me the mountain alders, which grow high in the rocks unlike alders that like their feet wet. He told me about hearing, on bitter winter nights, the crack of the frost splitting the trunks of trees, and he showed me how the bark of paper birches tends to darken and curl on northern and northeastern exposures.

He looked askance at me when I, a dweller in the Big Woods, said I had never enjoyed a snack of tender winter basswood buds.

He showed me how green twig-ends of cedars become brittle and fall in subzero winds, like manna for the deer. And he told me how, in his observations, a wolf attacks a deer at the side of the neck or shoulder and not, as is commonly claimed, at the hamstring. He told about finding himself, one day, in the middle of a pack of wolves that gave no attention to his presence, and of having the company of a pine marten while he worked in the woods.

He showed me how, without harming the trees, he gathers the bark of the paper birches for the paintings he makes. Sometimes, he said, he finds storm-loosened sheets on the ground after spring snowmelt.

He showed me the winter route that the wolves use when they travel up and down this ridge, and the route the red fox favors, which passes through a luxurious growth of caribou lichens on a rocky outcrop, now under drifted snow.

He stopped at a slight depression in the snow, exactly like a hundred others, so far as I could see, and told me that this is where the jack-in-the-pulpits, uncommon in these woods, bloom in the springtime. Even though they were covered with two to three feet of snow, he insisted that we walk around them.

He said he was following his old snowshoe trail. Once or twice he claimed to have lost it, although no trail was ever visible to me. After a while we emerged on a summit. Stunted firs and spruces grew on the rocky, wind-swept pinnacle. Some of the spruces were white spruces, some were black. Scherer handed me a bunch of needles from one of the trees and told me to crush them between my fingers. A sweet, clean, piney aroma erupted from them. "Black spruce," he said. "The needles of the white spruce don't give off that pleasant odor."

The mountain ended in a rock face that plunged eighty feet into a beaver pond. Forested hills washed away like waves in every direction to the horizon. Except for a communications tower on a distant hilltop, we might have believed we were at the heart of a trackless wilderness. In fact, we were almost literally in the shadow of a bustling ski resort and scarcely two miles from busy U.S. 61. Scherer pointed out the highest point in Minnesota, another hill, also called Eagle Mountain, some seventeen miles distant.

"I like to come here in the summer," he said, "away from the mosquitoes and dawdle over lunch on this rock and stretch out afterwards for a nap. Then I'm in heaven."

And then we went down through the long shadows of the afternoon, toward the world of commerce and noise. We went down and down and down, realizing as we descended how effortless the attractions of the forest had made the climb seem.

We paused only at a pair of parallel tracks in a maple grove. A snowshoe hare had passed through, a somewhat unusual event, Scherer said. "Hares don't normally like such open woods," he said. Then he pointed out that sometime later a pine marten had come along, tracking the hare. "If it were only earlier in the day," Scherer said, "we might follow those tracks and have another story to tell."

I drove the 250 miles home by the light of a full moon, thinking about the day in the woods and about Auden's remark, "A culture is not better than its woods." I thought that Scherer had taught me what Auden meant. I had come to see a woods, and Scherer had shown me not the woods, but the stories that the forest tells. And what is a culture if not an accumulation of stories, like the duff that collects on a forest floor? And what is the worth of a culture if it does not treasure those stories and pass them down from one generation to the next, as they have been treasured and passed down in the Lutsen woods?

What Is Old Growth?

It's not as simple as it might sound to determine which forests are old growth—and hence deserving of special attention. According to DNR guidelines, old-growth forests must usually be dominated by trees at least 120 years old and be essentially undisturbed, which means unaffected by catastrophes such as major windstorms or extensive logging.

Scientists usually begin to evaluate a forest by measuring tree trunks. A large diameter often signifies advanced age, but tree species, climate, and site conditions also affect the diameter a tree achieves. A 150-year-old sugar maple in a northern hardwood forest, for example, might reach 2½ feet in diameter, while a 150-year-old black spruce in a bog might stand only a few feet tall with a trunk a few inches wide.

An abundance of snags (standing dead trees) characterizes most old-growth communities—but not old-growth red pine forests because few red pines die before 150 years of age. Scientists also look for other features: many downed logs, a multilevel forest canopy, and canopy gaps left by fallen trees.

Old-growth maple-basswood and northern hardwood forests will support a rich, patchy understory, with species distributed according to the amount of sunlight reaching the forest floor. The understory typically includes a lively array of spring ephemerals such as Dutchman's-breeches and spring-beauties. In old-growth pine forests, however, the understory is relatively sparse and lacks spring ephemerals.

DNR scientists have been defining, locating, and protecting old-growth forests since the late 1980s. DNR forest ecologist Kurt Rusterholz estimates that before European settlement, old-growth stands made up about half of Minnesota forests. Today, he estimates, only 1 to 4 percent of the original extent of old-growth forest remains. Most of Minnesota's fifty thousand acres of old growth protected today is in the Boundary Waters Canoe Area Wilderness and Itasca State Park.

DNR and U.S. Forest Service guidelines are establishing a network of additional old-growth stands on state and federal land. But policies might easily change, in which case old growth would no longer be protected.

Photography

John Gregor: 2, 6, 10, 14, 18, 34, 38 left, 54, 58, 62, 66, 94, 120, 124, 126

Richard Hamilton Smith: 22, 30, 38 right, 98 right, 102

John Pennoyer: 26 left

Richard Haug: 26 right, 74, 90

Dominique Braud: 40, 44, 48, 110

Jim Gindorff: 70, 86

L.C. Duke: 78

Kelly Randall: 82

Dan Wovcha: 84

Bill Marchel: 98 left

Stephen Maxson: 106, 114, 118

Index